NATO in the 1960's

NATO

IN THE

1960's

The Implications of Interdependence

<small>REVISED EDITION</small>

ALASTAIR BUCHAN

FREDERICK A. PRAEGER
Publisher · New York

BOOKS THAT MATTER

Published in the United States of America in 1963 by
Frederick A. Praeger, Inc., Publisher
64 University Place, New York 3, N.Y.

This is a revised edition of the book first
published in 1960 by Frederick A. Praeger, New York.

Printed in the United States of America

CONTENTS

NATO in the 1960's

INTRODUCTION

When the Institute for Strategic Studies was founded in November, 1958, one of the principal objectives of those who brought it into being was to foster a series of independent appraisals of national or international strategic and military problems. The present scope and resources of the Institute do not permit it to undertake major projects of original research. But one useful service that it can render both to governments and to the public is to bring together groups of experienced minds to re-examine some of the accepted premises of existing policy and the factors that may affect them in the future. *NATO in the 1960's*, published in the spring of 1960 as the basis of a series entitled "Studies in International Security," was the Institute's first contribution of this kind.

The problem of interdependence has necessarily preoccupied in recent years the thoughts of anyone concerned with the future of the Western alliances. The process of clarifying and invigorating my own thoughts was greatly assisted by an international study group on this problem which met regularly at the Institute throughout the first eight months of 1959. This group included: Professor Max Beloff (Chairman), Professor of Government at Oxford; Jacques de Bourbon Busset; Sir Anthony Buzzard; Peter Calvocoressi, John Grant, the Defense Correspondent of *The Times*; Denis Healey, M.P.; Professor W. W. Rostow, now Director of the State Department's Policy Planning Staff; and Sir George Thomson, the eminent British scientist; as well as a number of other distinguished minds.

The draft of the study was then used as the principal working document at a private conference held at Oxford, under the Chairmanship of Marshal of the Royal Air Force Sir John Slessor. This conference was attended by more than a hundred experts, including civil and military officials of the NATO staffs and Secretariat and representatives of almost every NATO country.

I was most grateful to all members of the original study group and to the members of the Oxford conference for the time, energy, and thought they devoted to this problem—in particular, to Max Beloff and Sir John Slessor. However, this is not a committee or conference document, but rather one man's attempt to formulate the problems and the answers to some of them, aided by discussions which were the more stimulating since they did not always produce a unanimous view.

The Institute does not seek access to classified material, and this study is based almost entirely on documents that are generally available. However, it would have been impossible to gain much real insight into the problems that interdependence within NATO raises without access to the experience and judgments of many officials, civilian and military. The group owes a debt of gratitude to a number of people in official positions who gave us the benefit of their counsel and experience.

The three premises on which this study was founded are straight-forward enough, though their implications are not. The first is that, on the best assumption, the world is unlikely to reach a stage of *détente* and stability which will make it possible for the Western powers to dispense with NATO in the discernible future. This does not mean that there is no hope of an agreement on some aspects of arms control. What is assumed, nevertheless, is that a workable system of general disarmament will take a long time to negotiate and may be subject to many pitfalls and reverses; though any consideration of NATO's future policy and structure must bear disarmament clearly in mind, any idea that the Alliance can be dispensed with in the immediate future seems to be irresponsible and unwise. Moreover, as the dissensions between London, Washington, Bonn, and Paris since the Berlin crisis have illustrated, a more closely knit Western alliance is the necessary precondition of a relaxation of international tension, not an alternative to it.

The second is that the central problem that now confronts the North Atlantic Treaty nations—in default of progress toward disarmament—and that will confront them increasingly over the next ten years, is the diversification of the strength of the Soviet bloc into many new forms of military, economic, and political power. If it were merely the intensification of one particular form of strength or pressure—say, in missiles or in economic aid—the new form of Soviet challenge could perhaps be met by the means that served the Alliance during its first decade. But the problem that faces NATO during its second decade, that of developing flexibility and stability without sacrificing strength, is considerably more complex than that which confronted it during its first ten years.

The third premise is that the NATO countries will insist on retaining as much of their national sovereignty, in this new situation, as is compatible with the security and the flexibility of the Alliance as a whole. I have no illusions that any form of Atlantic federation will be practical politics during this decade, or even in the next. Nor is it likely that the concessions of sovereignty or freedom of action that the European members are prepared to make to the European Economic Community and its agencies would be made to NATO, which is essentially an alliance directed by an intergovernmental conference in permanent session, the NATO Council. Where I have suggested a more radical approach to the specialization of functions between different countries, or where new institutions are discussed, it is in practical terms to meet a specific problem. Interdependence may yet prove an inadequate answer to the challenge of the 1960's, but until its implications have been thoroughly explored, it is premature to talk of more drastic solutions.

Any consideration of the central problems of the Alliance rapidly takes one far outside the field of strategy and military planning. For the problem is as much political and economic as it is military. However, in order to keep this study within manageable compass, I considered it necessary to confine myself primarily to security policy, and to leave equally—perhaps more—important aspects of interdependence, such as trade policies or aid to underdeveloped countries, to those more qualified to study them. This is not a comprehensive examination of the problems confronting the West, but a study of one central component of a large problem. At the same time, it is impossible to consider the problem of interdependence and its implications without reference to the kind of military posture and strategic doctrine around which the Alliance can cohere.

So rapid is the pace of contemporary developments, political and technological, that much has happened in the past three years to overtake the judgments and outdate the facts that were put forward when this book was first published: The "missile gap" has given way to a clear American superiority in strategic nuclear weapons; Soviet pressure on Berlin has been intensified; the rise of the European Economic Community and Britain's decision to identify herself more closely with Europe are altering the balance of power within the Alliance even more rapidly than was foreseen; and the problems of technological interdependence between the Allies have become, if anything, harder to resolve.

I have therefore revised this book in order to take some account of these developments. But I would like to stress that, in doing so, I have not altered its central focus, in that it assumes a continuing and interdependent relationship between all the NATO Allies, rather than a nebulous "partnership" between a united Europe and the United States. Sometime in the next twenty years the Atlantic world may become regrouped around two great powers, roughly similar in power and effectiveness. But this is unlikely to happen during the decade in which we are living, and if it does, this book will be finally outdated. In the meantime, we cannot ignore the problems to which an interdependent relationship between the United States and her fourteen NATO Allies daily gives rise.

In preparing this revised edition, I have incorporated certain fresh ideas which I published in the January, 1962, issue of *Foreign Affairs* under the title "The Reform of NATO." In order to give the general reader an opportunity to reach his own assessment of the military balance between the Communist bloc and the Western alliances, and in order to avoid overloading the text of the book with figures, I have included the 1962–63 edition of the Institute's analysis of this balance as an Appendix.

A. B.

November, 1962

I
THE
NEED FOR
INTERDEPENDENCE

SOVIET MEANS AND SOVIET ENDS

I

This study is an attempt to clarify some of the problems that seem likely, from our present standpoint in time, to confront the governments and peoples of the fifteen NATO countries in the coming years. Consequently, some judgment on the trends of Soviet policy must be its starting point. The reason for this is a simple one: The North Atlantic Treaty Organization was called into being by fears of Soviet intentions toward Western Europe, and it has proved necessary to maintain and strengthen it because those fears have not yet been laid to rest—indeed, in the minds of some thoughtful people, they have become intensified. But NATO is not a world organization for collective security like the United Nations: it could not, for instance, intervene as the U.N. has done in the disputes of the Middle East or Africa. Nor is it designed to forestall or thwart every form of threat to the security of the free nations of Western Europe and North America: it could, for instance, play little part, as an alliance, in dealing with a fresh outbreak of belligerence on the part of China. For that purpose, other means and other coalitions exist, even though they involve several of the NATO countries. Though NATO's responsibilities have extended as Soviet power has extended, it is the confrontation of the central Soviet threat that is the primary function of the Alliance.

"I cannot forecast to you the action of Russia," said Sir Winston Churchill, in a broadcast in October, 1939. "It is a riddle wrapped in a mystery inside an enigma." This, like so many Churchillian phrases, seems a judgment that has come full circle, in that it has a greater ring of truth today than in the years immediately after it was uttered. There was a period in the late 1940's and early 1950's—the years of Azerbaidzhan, Czechoslovakia, the Berlin blockade, and Korea—when we thought we could discern a cruel consistency in Soviet policy, a ruthless determination to probe by all means short of total war those points where the West was weakest, in order to expand the territorial limits of Communist power. At a later period, a new thesis could be constructed, that Soviet policy was concentrated upon undermining by diplomatic and economic measures those Asian and Middle Eastern governments that had close relations with the West. Since 1955, the declared policy of the Soviet Union has been peaceful economic competition with the West, the ambition to prove to the rest of the world that the secret of dynamic economic growth has passed from the hands of the old capitalist societies into her own.

Yet, today, we feel more inclined to accept Churchill's sense of bafflement than to base Western policy upon any one analysis of Soviet policy. The reason we feel so unsure of our ground is that the gap between the declared aims of the Soviet Union as set forth by Mr. Khrushchev—economic competition and general disarmament—and Soviet military capabilities is now so wide that it is very difficult to know which to accept as our guide.

We know that the nature of Soviet society is changing all the time, becoming more bourgeois in its structure, less revolutionary in its aim. Still, there is a hardly diminished strain of pugnacity and suspicion in the whole Russian attitude toward the non-Communist world. We may presume that Mr. Khrushchev sincerely believes in the necessity for peaceful coexistence between capitalism and Communism. Yet the assumption of Marxist dialectic, that only the capitalists are capable of aggression, justifies continuous subversion of Western interests and the support of "wars of colonial liberation." We may believe that Mr. Khrushchev is a cautious man, but we know that he has gratuitously taken great risks over Berlin and Cuba.

There has been a constant debate throughout history as to whether the policy of one power toward another should be governed by the latter's intentions or capabilities. This debate has often dominated Western discussion of NATO policy. In the military sphere, the wisest course is probably to examine the adversary's capabilities first, and then to see what limitations are likely to govern their use—that is, to shape his intentions. To form a sound judgment, therefore, it is essential first to study the present military capabilities of the Soviet Union, for there is no country whose strategic position has been more profoundly transformed in the hectic fifteen years of change since V-E Day.

Ten years ago, Russia disposed of only one form of military challenge to the West, the Soviet Army in Europe. It is true that even then she had an excellent fighter-aircraft force in the making; it is also true that she possessed a sizable though somewhat antiquated submarine fleet. More important, her political power, reaching out through the appeal of Communism to the organized working class and to intellectuals of the war-shattered European countries, gave her an influence beyond her military strength. But she had no form of long-range striking power, and even though she successfully exploded an atomic bomb only four months after the signing of the Atlantic Treaty, it was the Red Army in Europe—vast, menacing, and cruel—that dominated the minds of those who set their signatures to it.

Ten years ago, Russia was a great military power only in the traditional sense of the word. Yet, in less than a decade, she has not only become immeasurably stronger, but has acquired a diversification of strength that a short time ago would have seemed beyond her grasp for at least a generation. This is now no more than a glimpse of the obvious, since the new forms of Soviet strength have been developing for all to see for at least five years. But it is useful, in order to see how complex is the problem that will confront the

NATO countries over the next decade, to break Soviet power down into its component parts, and then to attempt a rough assessment of how the Soviet leaders envisage employing these components.

II

There is no subject on which it is harder to keep a proper balance between caution and pessimism than the question of Soviet long-range striking power.

Since 1954, when the Soviet Union first displayed long-range bombers in quantity, the West has had to acknowledge that the Soviet Union has acquired a form of power which she has never before possessed in modern history—namely, long-range striking power. There is no doubt that the Soviet military leaders came to the conclusion, even before the dead hand of Stalin was relaxed, that a Soviet policy of deterrence in the nuclear age required an ability to threaten the United States as well as Europe. Only by this means could the already formidable American striking power and what Russians regard as the American bridgehead in their own continent—namely, the American forces in Germany and other European bases—be neutralized. The long-range striking power of the Soviets assumed a much more dramatic form when the first of their very large intercontinental missiles, on which they had been working since 1946 (long before they had mastered the atomic, let alone the hydrogen, bomb), was successfully fired in August, 1957. Within two years, it was clear that they were not only building up a dependable force of these big ICBM's, but also creating a formidable missile threat to Europe.

For several years after 1957, the Western appreciation of Soviet intentions in this field was, to say the least, faulty and mistaken. It was assumed, from estimates of Soviet industrial and scientific capacity, that she must be building up a large ICBM force with the object of achieving strategic superiority over the United States. During 1958–60, when the American missile program was only slowly gathering momentum, this belief created the mythological "missile gap," and American service leaders constantly reiterated their conviction that unless the United States embarked on a crash program of production, the Soviet Union would have a lead of at least 3 to 1 in ICBM's by about 1962. This fear of a Soviet quantitative superiority in ICBM's not only gave especial impetus to the programs for such American missiles as Polaris, Titan, and Minuteman; it also emphasized the permanent asymmetry between the Western and the Soviet strategic positions—namely, that the Soviet Union can protect her bases from attack by political means, that is, by secrecy about their locations, while in the open West, it is necessary to use costly mechanical forms of protection, "hardening," mobile sites, air-borne alerts, or submarines.

It is essential in the interests of stability that Western retaliatory bases continue to be made as invulnerable as possible, but the earlier preoccupation with a Soviet attempt to gain a numerical superiority over the United States was mistaken for three reasons. First, it has not happened. At present, it is doubtful that the Soviet Union has more than 75 ICBM's deployed, whereas the American figure has reached nearly 400–500 and will go beyond 1,000 by 1965–66.

Second, it overlooked the central difference between the American and the Soviet strategic positions in the world. The United States is committed to help protect forty-two allies in four continents. To uphold their morale and hold their loyalty, she has little option but to maintain a strategic striking force large enough to ensure that, in the event of war, the Soviet Union will suffer the maximum punishment, while America's allies, as well as her own citizens, will suffer the minimum punishment. Her position, as the center of a web of alliances, as the linchpin of the containment policy, forces her to develop a strategic force large enough to be able to destroy as many as possible of the sources of Soviet offensive power—a counter-force strategy. By comparison, the Soviet Union dominates all her allies except China and has a highly evolved political doctrine to enable her to "win friends and influence people" by means other than war. All that she requires of a strategic force is that it should deter attack on Russia itself, and for this purpose, she believes that a force that can threaten the major American cities and industrial areas is adequate. (This doctrine conveniently dovetails with her economic necessities and with the demands of her space program on her limited supply of scientific and skilled manpower.)

In the third place, preoccupation with the size of the Soviet ICBM force tends to divert attention from its nature. Ever since the Soviet Union resumed nuclear tests in August, 1961, it has been clear that she intended to use her lead in very large rockets to lift warheads of an enormous yield. One of more than 50 megatons has been tested, and Mr. Khrushchev boasted (to a World Peace Congress!) in July, 1962, of a 100-megaton bomb. Current Soviet strategic literature, in addition to making claims about antimissile defenses, now lays emphasis on the colossal destruction over vast areas that a modern war would involve. There can be little doubt that at a time when the United States is trying to create a more flexible system of deterrence, the Soviet Union is putting its main emphasis on terror weapons, hoping to cow the NATO countries in an emergency by the specter of wholesale destruction of their cities and industrial areas.

If the deterrence of attack by the United States is based on a small force of ICBM's of great destructive power, the Soviet leaders retain enough of their traditional fear of invasion to employ both a psychological and an active military deterrent in relation to their close neighbors. In contrast to her small number of ICBM's, she has deployed some 600 medium-range missiles targeted on Western Europe and about 100 targeted on Japan. These could pose a devastating threat not only to European cities but also to NATO military installations, bases, airfields, and communications. By this means, as Mr. Khrushchev has made clear in his conversations with various Western visitors, the Soviet Union intends not only to demonstrate to Europe that it is at her mercy, but also, if need be, to destroy the sources of potential attack on the Soviet Union.

Russia is a power that, until the end of World War II, was virtually invulnerable from the sea and is still virtually independent of sea-borne imports. Yet she maintains the second largest navy in the world, measured in terms of tonnage. Apart from its force of 20 cruisers, the Soviet Navy has some 410 submarines (the total number has recently been reduced from about 450), 300 of which are long-range, divided between the Arctic, the Baltic, the Black Sea, and the Far East fleets. Ten of these are nuclear-propelled.

It is very doubtful if anyone in authority in Russia today could give a consistent reason why such a huge submarine fleet has been amassed and maintained. Certainly no democratic politician could have escaped the scrutiny of the budget that it entails, and Khrushchev, during his first two years of office, gave every indication of trying to cut it down. The submarine program was laid down in the Stalinist years, when the U.S. was still inviolable and any major war would have involved the detachment or subjugation of the forward bases of SAC—that is, Britain, Iceland, and the other members of what is now NATO—by every possible means, including starvation by a devastating battle of the Atlantic.

A program geared to a central strategic concept is not easily reversed, even when the concept becomes obsolete. There is evidence to show that Khrushchev's accession to power coincided with (or perhaps followed) a major reappraisal of the Soviet submarine program. The Soviet Naval Staff developed two fresh lines of thought, which had clearly been maturing during the Stalinist years, to justify its existence. The first was the immense nuisance value of the Soviet submarine in non-Soviet hands. The Vladivostok Soviet fleet numbers 120 submarines: as a Russian force, it could not take part in the Korean War; but if there had been even 6 "North Korean" submarines, the logistic task of the United Nations fleets would have been enormously complicated. Consequently, there are now more than 20 Soviet submarines in the Mediterranean flying other flags. And the process of distributing submarines to countries unfriendly to the West will presumably continue. One does not have to predicate any form of "broken-backed warfare," as many Soviet admirals and their Western counterparts were once inclined to do, to envisage a very fruitful field of troublemaking for the

Soviet submarines. The fact, for instance, that no NATO power could sail a convoy through the Mediterranean, around the Cape, or through the Java Straits to meet some limited war situation (in which the Soviet Union might ostensibly not be involved) without full antisubmarine deployment could mean a difference of hundreds of thousands of hours in labor and time.

But the Soviet Navy is hydra-headed, for few nations have ever had the opportunity to turn a doubtful strategic asset to such good advantage. The Soviet Union has been slower than the United States to develop nuclear submarines, and it was probably not before the summer of 1962 that she successfully fired a true Polaris-type submerged missile. Hitherto, her quite efficient surface-fired submarine missiles have been adequate to pose a *threat* to the crowded littorals of North America and Western Europe, and, indeed, to the previously inviolate areas of the Southern Hemisphere. As the American Polaris fleet grows, the Soviet nuclear hunter-killer submarines, of which there may be twenty by the end of 1964, can embarrass its operations and movements. At the same time, if the Russians become seriously concerned with the problem of the vulnerability of their land missile bases, as they appear to be already, they can accelerate their own Polaris-type program.

The army is the traditional expression of Soviet power, not merely because Russia is a land-locked country, but because the particular form of power that ground force is capable of wielding— the seizing and securing of terrain, cities, industries, provinces—occupied a well-defined place in Leninist thought. Between 1960 and 1961, it looked as if Soviet policy was going to follow the course that was pursued first in American and later in British defense policy—namely, to absorb the increasing cost of strategic weapons systems by reductions in mobilized manpower. But the decision of January, 1960, to reduce manpower by one-third was reversed within eighteen months. Consequently, the dispositions and strength of the Soviet Army have not varied greatly in the last ten years. Until about 1955, it was 3 million strong and now it is about 2.5 million. It consists of some 160 divisions (as against an earlier figure of 175), of which some 20 are armored, 50 are infantry, while the rest are being converted to motorized divisions with a reasonable degree of mobility. Twenty of these divisions—10 armored, 10 motorized—are stationed in East Germany; 6 more are in Poland and Hungary, while behind them stand 75 divisions in European Russia in various degrees of training and readiness. Some 60 divisions belonging to the European satellites (principally Czechoslovakia, Poland, and Romania) have little mobility or offensive power, and in the event of war, those that did not evaporate would be used to guard the long lines of Russian communications. This arithmetic, which has mesmerized the NATO powers for so many years, conceals, however, more than it reveals. For it is the improved quality of these forces that is of importance. The 20 armored and motorized divisions in East Germany, many of them equipped with new tanks and a new 120-mm. gun, are not an occupation but an operational force. The tactical air force which supports them is the most up-to-date branch of the Soviet Air Force. In addition, there are 10 air-borne divisions in the Soviet Army, with a simultaneous airlift for two divisions. Though the Soviet Army is by no means irrevocably committed to the use of tactical atomic weapons, they are now standard equipment, and the Army, after a late start, has laid very great emphasis over the past five years on training for movement and attack on the nuclear battlefield.

One reason why it proved so difficult to apply technological advances to the strengthening of the NATO powers was the fact that the Korean War forced them to go into a crash production program of, for the most part, World War II types of equipment. Democratic budgetary processes being what they are, it has been very difficult to allocate money for new equipment until these stocks have been run down or worn out. As the aggressor, and knowing just how far she intended to commit herself in the Korean War, Russia was not confronted with the same problem; and in so far as she has had surplus stocks, she has found it easy to unload them on the satellite armies. Consequently, the Soviet divisions in East Germany, and some of those behind them, must be regarded soberly as the best equipped and among the most highly trained forces in the world. In terms of quality, they can be matched only by the U.S. Seventh Army in Germany, which they outnumber four to one. However, the reconstruction of the Soviet ground forces and their increased mobility have also made them more roadbound, more vulnerable to interdiction, and much less like the Tartar horde that swept westward in 1944–45.

This brief sketch by no means encompasses the whole of the diversity of the Soviet effort, even in the military field. For ten years, the amount of effort that has gone into air defenses has been very considerable. There is a striking emphasis in all Soviet writing on the great importance of active air and missile defenses. Soviet defense expenditure is nominally about $14.7 billion (1962) and is estimated in real terms at about $33 billion, less than two-thirds that of the United States. But there is probably less waste of resources in the Soviet defense effort than in that of the United States, and greater emphasis on the development and production of larger quantities of fewer overlapping types of planes and other weapons than is the case within NATO as a whole.

III

But the mere cataloguing of military hardware is no real guide to the intentions of a nation. What, in fact, are the underlying assumptions of this remarkable diversity of military power that the Soviet Union has achieved in so short a time?

Few people would argue that the Soviet Union is planning a deliberate and cold-blooded assault upon the NATO powers, in the sense that Hitler had made up his mind by the beginning of 1937 that war was in the German interest. No country has more to gain from peace over the next decade than the Soviet Union, and no one is more aware of this than the present generation of Soviet leaders—Khrushchev, Mikoyan, and the rest—whose reputations were made in the reconstruction of Soviet industry and civilization from the smoking rubble that the Germans left behind. A man's accomplishments are not only his monument, but also his emotional anchor. The estimates of those Western strategic analysts who believe that the present Soviet leaders can face a degree of damage to the Soviet Union which the West cannot contemplate for itself (for the reason that the Russians suffered an enormous degree of destruction in World War II and yet survived) overlook the fact that for Khrushchev and his colleagues, the raw new industrial agglomerations of the Moscow, Leningrad, or Kiev areas have as deep a significance as Coventry, Rheims, or Philadelphia have for us.

What purpose, then, does this vast apparatus of Soviet military power, achieved with so much sacrifice and retardation of economic growth, really serve? If aggressive nuclear war against the West has been largely ruled out of Soviet calculations, by fear of the destruction it would provoke against the Soviet Union itself, does the continuing size of the Soviet Army and the Soviet Navy mean that a nonnuclear war with the West is a realistic option for Moscow? Certainly the writings of the Soviet General Staff suggested that the idea had not been discarded until about 1959 or 1960. Nuclear warfare was only reluctantly assimilated into Soviet strategic thought, for since the essence of Communist doctrine is the need for the transformation of societies, so cataclysmic a weapon ill serves their purpose. But, despite the preoccupation of some Soviet military writers with nonnuclear global war, there is nothing in the declarations of the Soviet leaders to suggest that that is a situation they would welcome or foster. It remains one of a number of options open to them in a given situation, but no more.

However, the role of Russian force as an agent of change in the world has been a consistent thread in Soviet doctrine for over forty years. But there has always been one very important condition attached to its use—namely, that the Red Army exists not to conquer other countries, but to exploit and consolidate domestic revolution once it has been fomented by other means. Originally, it was Lenin's hope that Communist regimes could be established in the European countries by this means, and Stalin was able to accomplish it by exploiting the power vacuum created by Nazi conquest and withdrawal in the countries immediately bordering on the Soviet Union. Stalin's purpose was, undoubtedly, to carry this success a stage further by encouraging a split between the major Western powers. This the foundation of NATO has so far prevented his successors from doing, while the successful defiance of Tito demonstrated for all the world to see the existing limitations of this kind of political-military strategy.

In recent years, it has been possible to discern an application of the same techniques in Southeast Asia and in the Middle East, though the menace of nuclear war has made the Soviet attempts to exploit situations of civil unrest more tentative and more cautious.* There is no reason, however, to assume that the policy has been relegated forever to the archives of the Kremlin—as, for instance, the hypothesis of war with France was relegated to the archives of Whitehall in the early 1900's—or that it would not be refurbished if Russia ever had reason again to think that the advantages could possibly outweigh the risks.

There is no doubt that, for the time being, the Soviet leaders have set economic competition with the West as one of their foremost declared objectives, even if the Soviet economy has taken something of a setback in the last two years. And there is obviously much to attract them to such a policy: the aspirations of the new Soviet bureaucratic middle class; the growing gap in living standards between the developed and the underdeveloped countries of the world; the attractions of Communist economic methods to nations trying to overcome the lapse of centuries; and, for that matter, the stultification of more direct means of challenging the West. There can be little doubt that one of Mr. Khrushchev's dreams is of a

---

* For example: the equivocal and lukewarm support given to Colonel Kassim in Iraq; the failure to back up the Vietnamese guerrillas in 1961; and the hasty withdrawal of Soviet "technicians" from the Congo in 1960. Only in Cuba has the Soviet Union considered the gains from a Communist bridgehead in the American sphere of influence to be worth the risk of treading near the brink of war, and even there, a display of American firmness in October, 1962, led to the rapid withdrawal of their offensive weapons.

Russia that is not only the economic hub of the universe—a sort of latter-day Cobdenite England—but also the lodestar of the uncommitted world, because with its virtues of discipline and hard work it displays a superior morality to the hedonist and confused capitalist societies of the old world. The historic Russian desire has been to protect itself from infection with Western values. Mr. Khrushchev is the first Russian leader with the assurance to believe that Russia can assert its own values to the world.

But Soviet pressure on Berlin refutes any simple assumption that Russia has decided to recast her relations with the West in completely new terms. Clearly, one new factor of great importance is that the Soviet leaders have been delivered, mostly by their own prowess, from the trauma of Russian military inferiority, which dates back not just to 1917 but to ancestral Russia. This trauma was probably, in our generation, most acute in the years just before and after Stalin's death, when it was clear that the United States possessed a sufficiency of nuclear bombs, plus bombers and overseas bases, to inflict a crippling degree of damage on the Soviet Union, to which she could not reply in kind. The steady growth in the confidence of Soviet diplomacy during the past five years has, by the admission of Soviet leaders, been partly grounded on the growth of her ability, first to inflict swift damage on Western Europe, then to deliver a crippling blow on most of the overseas bases of SAC, and finally to threaten the cities and bases in the United States itself.

IV

If this release from fear of attack were final and absolute, the end of a historic nightmare, it should have had a stabilizing effect on Soviet policy, particularly since Soviet actions are so much more cautious than their words. But to argue that, because the Soviet Union has become a great military power in every respect, her leaders are now, as they claim, primarily preoccupied with peaceful competition with the West overlooks three facts.

The first is that concentration on economic growth and economic

aid does not constitute an alternative to the continuing development of military strength for an economy the size of Russia's—any
more than it does for the United States. There is no doubt that
many aspects of the Soviet military budget now form a serious drain
on the economy, particularly the large amount of manpower that is
maintained in uniform. There can be little doubt that Mr. Khrushchev was profoundly disappointed when his announcement of a
one-third cut in Soviet military manpower in 1960 (which, in the
event, was not carried out) did not lead to equivalent Western
reductions. It is one of the reasons why his disarmament proposals
may well be constructed around a core of genuine and urgent national self-interest. Nevertheless, Soviet economic aid to the underdeveloped countries—that is, the external use of Soviet economic
power—is at present on a small scale and constitutes only a fraction
of the military budget.

The second point is that the Soviet leaders have no apparent interest, at present, in a stable relationship with the West. For the
real advantage that their position of nuclear parity affords them is
their growing freedom to encourage what Khrushchev paradoxi-
cally described to Walter Lippmann as the *status quo*, by which he
meant the social and economic revolutions taking place in Latin
America, Asia, Africa, and the Middle East. Piecing together his
statements, it is clear that one use of the vast apparatus of Soviet
military power will be to deter the West from any form of resist-
ance to or interference with Russia's ambition to become the political and economic leader of that great majority of the world's
population who are not members of mature industrial democratic
societies. Her military power is thus the essential basis of her policy
of economic and political competition. Moreover, since 1961, when
they resumed nuclear testing in defiance of neutral protests, the
Soviet leaders seem to have lost their earlier interest in gaining the
good will of the uncommitted. Berlin does not, of course, much
interest the uncommitted world. But the building of the wall in
August, 1961, and the threats that have accompanied the attempts
to bully the Western powers out of the city have considerably

jeopardized the Soviet "image" of a peaceful power taking only reasonable precautions against attack by neurotic capitalists.

Finally, there is the intractable problem presented by the inherent instability of a system of mutual deterrence between the Soviet Union and NATO that is based primarily on missiles as the means of delivering nuclear warheads. If Russian intentions now embrace a preventive war against the West—a bolt from the blue one Sunday afternoon—one would not expect to find any sign of it in their writings or statements. But it must seem even to the most pessimistic a very improbable contingency, and one so damaging to Soviet relations with the rest of the world, in terms of fallout alone, that, even if Russia could lay most of the still distrusted and despised West in ashes at a single blow, her statesmen would recoil from doing so.

The real problem is different. It arises from the fact that, in the missile age, the man who strikes first has an overwhelming advantage in terms of ability to inflict damage without suffering the equivalent in retaliation, unless his adversary has taken enormously costly preparations to render his own means of retaliation "hard"— that is, relatively invulnerable to nuclear attack—by putting his aircraft and missiles underground or at sea. It is this that has created the Russian strategists' preoccupation with the conceivable necessity of making a "pre-emptive strike" in a period of tension— that is to say, of striking first because intelligence or radar information convinces you that your adversary is on the point of striking you. The most obvious source of tension would be any form of limited war. The rapid strides that have been made to improve the invulnerability of Western means of retaliation—SAC's air-borne alert system, the Polaris submarine, the Minuteman program—have removed the worst of these fears. But no unilateral action can deal with the problems of accident, of miscalculating the adversary's motives in a period of tension, or of escalation from a low level of conflict to a strategic exchange once war has started.

It is possible that both sides will soon recognize the dangers of this situation, and will succeed in mastering it by an agreement on measures of safeguard against surprise attack or miscalculation, at least in Europe. So far, their efforts have been fruitless, and the technical obstacles are still formidable. Remote though the possibility of accidental war may be, its very direness is enough to poison Soviet-NATO relations, for the characteristics of the missile undermine the factors otherwise making for stability in an age of nuclear stalemate.

There remains the obscure and difficult question of Soviet-Chinese relations, of Russia's own problem of interdependence. In terms of Russia's relations with NATO, China is both an asset and a liability at the same time; or perhaps it would be truer to say that she has been an asset and may now be judged a liability. She has been an asset because she has, at various times in the past ten years, been able to subject the Alliance to serious strains by dividing the United States, in terms of both policy and public opinion, from her European allies—over Korea, over Indochina, over Formosa, and over Quemoy. Since Soviet thought has not yet freed itself from the Leninist view that the West can be made to fall apart in internecine strife, this is a high qualification in an ally.

But the continuing pugnacity of China, as exemplified by her attitude to India, is now out of step with the Soviet policy of peaceful coexistence and economic competition. The Soviet leaders are very well aware that wars between great powers have in the past developed against their will, that they have been drawn into them by the intransigence of allies. Quite apart from the doctrinal feud between the two countries, many Soviet statements—notably Mr. Khrushchev's speech in Peking in September, 1959, immediately after his return from the United States—have seemed to be intended to convey a clear warning to China: "Do not involve me in a war I do not seek." This speech alone should give cause for thought to those who see an advantage for the West in fomenting a Soviet-Chinese quarrel, for it is a delusion to hope that it would rescue NATO from its own problems, or do anything but heighten the chances of international disaster. Many Western students of Soviet policy now believe that the pressure on Berlin represents an attempt to iron out Russia's worst European headache, the position and status of East Germany, and to secure her western flank, before engaging in an even fiercer controversy with China over both conflicting doctrine and conflicting interests. It is from such secondary moves that great wars have often started in the past.

An analysis of the strategic intentions of a power so secretive as Russia is, at best, only a very rough guess, and it is foolish to attempt to define those intentions with any precision or to base Western calculations on any one speech or collection of writings. For all one can say with any certainty is that Russian policy is never dominated by any one single objective. As one eminent Western Soviet expert has put it: "Their idea is to set out three or four alternative policies and see what they can get." By the same token, no policy is ever dropped if it proves unsuccessful; it is merely shelved for the time being. In consequence, the most important fact that the NATO powers must confront about the Soviet Union today is not Soviet missile prowess, the efficiency of the Red Army, steel production, or economic aid, but the great range of options that are now open to Mr. Khrushchev. If the international weather remains sunny, he can press ahead with his policy of economic competition; if it darkens, he has the full apparatus of military power with which to adopt, overnight, as he recently did over Berlin, a far more menacing posture toward NATO than Stalin ever could. Consequently, it is the achievement of an equivalent flexibility that is the central task he has imposed upon NATO in its second decade.

But if Russian policy is not centered on any one objective, some aims can be pursued with greater subtlety and consistency than others. One of these is the isolation of the Atlantic world from the evolving nations of Asia, Africa, and Latin America. Much of the success of the propaganda about "Western imperialism" in these areas rests on a common sense of resentment that a group of countries that covers less than one-seventh of the globe's land surface and contributes little more than one-sixth of its population should still arrogate to itself the leadership of the world. The Russians are well aware of the strong hold that Western methods and ideals have in Asia and Africa, of traditions of jurisprudence and civil organization which they can undermine but cannot challenge. It is, therefore, greatly to their interest to portray the NATO powers themselves as a collection of nervous, fear-ridden communities lacking the sense of common purpose that they claim.

Another is to divide the Atlantic world itself. If the new Europe should deduce from its success in achieving economic unity that it could thereby be a new great power, independent of the United States, with the ability to pursue independent foreign and strategic policies, or if the United States should come to feel that the risks of helping to defend Europe were too high, then the Soviet leaders would have won, by their own reckoning, a prize of incalculable value.

2

THE MILITARY REQUIREMENTS
OF THE 1960's

I

In order to reach any sound conclusions about what steps NATO should take in this changed situation, it is not enough merely to assess the intentions or capabilities of the Soviet Union. Though NATO is a defensive alliance, it does not exist merely in order to react to Soviet policy, for the countries that compose it have legitimate objectives of their own. It is perhaps useful to remember that the North Atlantic Treaty has an initial life of only twenty years—that is, until 1969. Thus the Treaty has run more than half its life, and, in consequence, we have a definite span of time ahead of us in which to measure how far we have advanced toward these objectives.

Obviously, the aims of fifteen individual nations must comprise a catalogue so diverse as to be far outside the scope of this study. But, in their corporate life as members of the Alliance, I think there would be general agreement that the positive aims of NATO are fourfold. The first is, obviously, to prevent war of any kind from erupting, not just in Europe but anywhere in the hemisphere. To say that NATO is concerned with the prevention of general or nuclear war is not enough, for the consequences of even a limited exchange are too dangerous to accept.

The second is to contain the expansion of Russian influence throughout the world, until that element in Soviet policy that is grounded on xenophobic fear and dislike of the West is reduced to a minimum—in other words, to edge Soviet foreign policy closer to more constructive ends than the subversion and demolition of legitimate Western interests.

The third is to create the conditions in which it may be possible to contemplate the liquidation of NATO itself as a military organization by the negotiation of a better system of European security than that which exists today.

The fourth is to develop those institutions that adequately reflect, and satisfactorily reconcile, the diverse interests of both the European and the North American members of the Alliance.

Remote and daunting as these objectives are, they are limited. Their attainment would usher in no new millennium. Soviet distrust of Western capitalist society may take generations to die out completely, and many aspects of the Cold War—the fight, for instance, for the loyalties of the new nationalisms—may continue in some form for a long time. NATO as such can probably do very little to bring about a decrease of tension between China and the West, let alone to supersede any of the functions of the United Nations. But even the partial attainment of these objectives would be an achievement of vast importance. The mere prosecution of deterrent strategy and the maintenance of a divided Europe—however healthy and dynamic its Western half may be—are not sufficiently inspiring objectives to maintain the cohesion of so diverse a group of nations. If an ambitious political aim does not govern NATO's second decade, its purpose will be infirm, the tension between its various members will grow, and its strategic and military planning will be a hand-to-mouth affair.

Roughly equated, these aims of containment, of helping to build the basis for a European settlement, and of uniting the interests of the Atlantic powers correspond, in terms of NATO's military planning, to the ability to meet the "ambiguous" threat, to deter aggression in Europe, and to maintain a strategic balance of power.

II

The most ill-defined problem of the three is the "ambiguous" threat. This is the situation created by Soviet or Chinese encouragement—economic, political, or military—to revolutionary movements either in a NATO country or in one with whom the NATO powers have close relations; or by the breakdown of civil government and order in a free country or a colony, when the Communist powers are *tertius gaudens* even if they were not the prime instigators: a Vietnam or Cuba on the one hand, an Algeria or Congo on the other. The essential character of these "ambiguous" threats is that they may involve no overt act of Soviet or Chinese military hostility against a NATO power, and yet be highly destructive to the position of the NATO powers as a whole.

This has been the classic instrument of Soviet policy, and despite Moscow's greater self-confidence that she can now "win friends and influence people" by more open means, there is no reason to think that a tactic so deeply embedded in two generations of Leninist thought will be abandoned overnight when opportunity offers.

The problem of containing the ambiguous Communist threat has never been an exclusively military one. Moreover, there are few, if any, areas within NATO itself (northern Greece is perhaps one) where direct Communist subversion or the infiltration of volunteers is likely to appeal to Moscow's sense of caution. The principal danger lies outside the NATO area—in Africa, the Middle East, Asia, and Latin America. And the principal means by which the clear ambitions of China and Russia to extend their influence in these areas can be countered is intelligent liberal economic and political policies on the part of the NATO powers. It is the scope and breadth of the Communist challenge in the world that has changed since the idea of containment was first evolved in the years immediately after World War II. But containment need not be primarily a military policy, and the fact that there is now a greater emphasis on economic and social assistance in the Communist challenge has

made it essential for the West to respond even more in economic
and political terms.

But this does not mean that military force has no role to play in
discouraging such "ambiguous" threats or in countering them if
they occur. A brigade of seasoned troops, air-landed within thirty-six
hours of a request for help from some hard-pressed government—
whether a NATO or SEATO member or some other nation in the
free world—may redress a tense situation in a way that sixty battalions could not do a month later. Yet speed in itself is not the only
requirement: If the Western countries cannot demonstrate that
they are able to back up any intervention they might be requested
to make with a rapid follow-up of stronger forces than those that
can be airlifted immediately, it is doubtful if their help would be
sought in the first place. The limitations of strategic mobility are
as well understood by the uncommitted nations as by the two
principal adversaries. It is because the "ambiguous" threat seems
one of the most probable contingencies that will face the NATO
powers in the next decade that one must set a very high priority on
the development of mobile reserves within NATO as a principal
requirement of the 1960's. The development of a mobile striking
force, with contributions from eight NATO countries, has been
one of the most encouraging achievements of recent years in the
evolution of Alliance military policy.

But before leaving the question of subversion and the dangers
that are related to it, it is important to enter three *caveats*. If the
real world of tomorrow need not necessarily be that of H. G. Wells,
neither is it likely to be that of Rudyard Kipling. The ambitions
of the Soviet Union and China are not going to be contained
merely by the existence of such limited mobile reserves as the
NATO powers can muster. In the first place, the most likely trouble
spots are outside the NATO area, so that there is little prospect of
NATO itself either being called upon or being in a position to take
collective action. It is more a question of NATO in its own planning encouraging those member countries that are most likely to
be called upon—and this means Britain, France, and the United

States—to develop such reserves, even if this involves readjusting the collective burden of European defense. Fortunately, the Kennedy Administration has taken this problem very seriously as far as American policy on aid is concerned. Similarly, the end of the Algerian war has now enabled France to reorganize her armed forces on a long-term plan that makes provision for such a mobile *force d'intervention*. Although the British strategic reserve is now primarily committed to NATO, it still has an effective dual capability, as the Kuwait emergency of 1961 demonstrated. Secondly, and for the same reason, the NATO powers may well have as strong an interest in strengthening the police functions of the United Nations as they do in developing their own answer to the problem. The success which the late Dag Hammarskjöld had in the late 1950's in the Middle East, in nipping "ambiguous" situations in the bud before they could develop into real trouble, was remarkable. Similarly, the Congo emergency illustrated that there are certain situations that only the U.N. can handle, even if its organization and operations are much clumsier than those of the Western powers. Its activities have been bedeviled by the failure of most of the United Nations members to provide the necessary financial support, and it is a sad reflection on the political unity of NATO that some of its member nations resist their financial obligations as fiercely as do the Communist powers.

Finally, it must be remembered that the military aspect of a general policy of containment is today wholly conditioned by the over-all strategic balance at all levels. Neither China nor the Soviet Union will be greatly deterred from encouraging aggression or civil unrest if it knows that the NATO powers have no means of succor below the level of total war. That was the bitter lesson of Indochina in 1954. And the two Communist powers would be equally indifferent if they could calculate that the Soviet Union had acquired a firm strategic superiority over the United States, or that the United States would not act in concert with her principal allies as was briefly the case at Suez. The one consideration does not exclude the other, and it is because of the subtlety and dynamism of Communist political action that the United States has felt constrained to maintain a strategic superiority. One can hope that no one will ever again dare to move more than a pawn on the international chess board. But that hope depends entirely on the positions of the kings and queens.

III

Despite the new emphasis that has been placed on the importance of the "ambiguous" threat and on training and organization of the forces of the major NATO powers to meet it, there is no question that it is the defense of Europe that will continue to be the central preoccupation of the Alliance. At various times in the thirteen years since NATO was founded, it has seemed that the center of East-West tension was about to shift from Europe to the Far East or elsewhere. Perhaps when China becomes an important military power again, and if this should induce the Soviet Union to reach certain limited agreements with the West over Berlin and Germany, or to reduce the level of armaments in Europe, the spotlight may shift away from Europe. But this is unlikely during the next few years or even during this decade. Despite the fact that ICBM's can span the top of the world in half an hour, or that both the superpowers now have the ability to destroy each other's civilization from bases on their own national territory, it is Europe, the peninsula of the Eurasian mainland, where both sides most fear that the spark of war may ignite.

The consistent difficulty that has confronted NATO is to evolve any doctrine for the defense of Western Europe that does not involve either its conquest or its annihilation in the event of war. This difficulty has been compounded in recent years by the fact that the rise of Soviet intercontinental strategic power means that for the United States actively to threaten the use of its own strategic retaliatory power to protect Europe also involves the potential destruction of the great American cities and industrial areas and the loss of perhaps 80 million American lives. And the evolution of a common doctrine has been made much harder in the last two years by serious misunderstandings between the United States and her European allies.

As Mr. Robert Osgood has pointed out in his recent book *NATO: The Entangling Alliance,** there was an unresolved ambiguity in the idea upon which NATO was founded. It was conceived, at one and the same time, as a unilateral guaranty of the security of Europe by its most powerful member, the United States —which in 1949 possessed a complete monopoly of nuclear weapons—and as a collective-security pact in which every nation pulled its weight on the assumption that Europe would eventually become responsible for its own security.

A brief backward glance illustrates how these ideas have fluctuated in emphasis and now to a certain extent conflict. In the years immediately after the foundation of NATO, the Alliance was conceived both in Europe and in the United States as a unilateral guarantee of an American strategic strike on Russia if she moved farther westward in Europe. Then, in 1951 and 1952, came the full strain of the Korean War on American resources, and with it, the fear that Russia would exploit the opportunity of American military entanglement in Asia to attack Europe. It was decided to set up a full-scale military command in Europe (SHAPE), with General Eisenhower as its first commander; and, in February, 1952, the new NATO Council approved a rearmament program that called for the provision of 96 divisions (some 50 of them for a central area) and 9,000 aircraft by 1954. The concept of collective defense was accepted.

But in the years immediately thereafter, three developments reversed this emphasis on the collective defense of Western Europe. The first was the evidence that the NATO governments simply could not honor their commitments to develop so large a force. The European economies were only just beginning to recover under the stimulus of the Marshall Plan, and since Soviet policy had begun to lose its ruthless central direction with the death of Stalin in 1953,

* University of Chicago Press, 1962.

the European governments, faced with the choice of economic recovery or major rearmament to protect themselves, chose the
former. The second development was the decision of the Republican Administration, elected in November, 1952, rapidly to augment
American strategic striking power and to reassert its will to use it
for the protection of its allies—the so-called "massive retaliation"
doctrine. In the light of this, if Russian aggression of any scale in
Europe was to be met by an immediate American retaliatory blow,
it was difficult for the other NATO governments to see what purpose there was in building up conventional forces in Europe except
as a "tripwire" for American action. Third, the United States decided in 1954 to make available to its allies small nuclear weapons
for use against battlefield targets. It was assumed that these gave
a natural advantage to the defense and would enable a relatively
small force in Europe to hold back a numerically superior one.

In 1957, therefore, the NATO plan for European defense was
completely revised to provide thirty divisions for the central area,
equipped with tactical nuclear support. It was made clear that the
role of this force was not to resist Soviet aggression by itself, but to
act as a buffer that could clearly identify the Soviet action either as
some irresponsible decision by a satellite or by a junior Soviet commander or as deliberate aggression, and to impose a "pause" until
strategic action could be prepared and the Soviets confronted with
the risks to themselves of carrying aggression further. It was assumed, for the purposes of this plan, that the use of tactical nuclear
weapons in Europe would not necessarily lead to the use of strategic
weapons, and that a nuclear conflict could be confined to the battlefield.

For a year or so after the development of the revised plan, known
as MC70, this formula for the defense of Europe commanded general assent. But in the last two or three years, the conception has
become increasingly open to debate. In the first place, the target
figure of thirty divisions has not been reached. In the autumn of
1962, the force in the central area stood at twenty-four divisions,
and was to reach twenty-six divisions when all twelve German di-

visions were fully operational. The refusal of the United Kingdom to station the equivalent of more than three divisions in Europe, and of France, whose forces are being reorganized, to commit to NATO more than two of the six divisions she will now maintain on the Continent, make it unlikely that the force will grow much larger.

More important is the difference in European and American perspectives which the dispute about the size of these forces and their equipment has revealed. In the mid-1950's, the Eisenhower Administration was not particularly concerned about the level of ground forces since it was official doctrine that the American strategic striking force would deter any form of aggression. However, as the United States has become more vulnerable to Soviet strategic attack since the ICBM became a reality in 1957, she has very naturally had to admit that the stakes for which she would resort to strategic nuclear war must rise. There has never been any deviation from the basic American position that a full-scale Soviet aggression against Western Europe would invoke American strategic retaliation, however much damage the United States itself suffered in return. But clearly, the ability of the United States to consider invoking a strategic exchange against, say, a Soviet raid on the Denmark Straits, a grab for some minor objective in Germany or the Balkans, or a defiance of the Montreux Convention in the Dardanelles—some Soviet attempt to humiliate rather than conquer NATO—must decline. It has been increasingly accepted in the United States that to rely solely on the strategic threat is to invite such humiliation.

At the same time, intensive study and research concerning the likely developments on a battlefield where tactical nuclear weapons were used has led the American planners to two conclusions: first, that it is not true that tactical nuclear weapons necessarily favor the defense, since they involve dispersed tactics and a high turnover of manpower. Now that the Soviet Army is fully equipped with them, the favorable military differential that they once gave to NATO has disappeared. Secondly, the line between strategic and tactical nuclear weapons is very hard indeed to draw. Attempts to evolve a watertight doctrine of limited nuclear war—clear limitations of objectives that would be honored by both sides—have not stood up to the test of debate and analysis. Consequently, there has been a growing conviction in American and British military circles that the use of the very first nuclear weapon, however small, might rapidly "escalate" into a strategic exchange.* But if small nuclear weapons are in the hands of forward commanders, as the MC70 plan envisaged, they will inevitably be used if these forward units are in danger of being overrun, however careful the arrangements or however tightly the nominal chain of authority for their use may be drawn.

The consequence has been that since about 1959, the United States has applied increasing pressure to her European allies to strengthen their conventional forces and to place less reliance on tactical nuclear weapons. The Kennedy Administration has, since the spring of 1961, accentuated this pressure, and some of its spokesmen have unofficially advocated a wholly conventional defense system for Europe.

The European view on these matters has been going through an almost exactly contrary process of change. In the first place, it has proved difficult for the European countries to expand their conventional forces at a time of rapid economic growth and when their governments have much heavier burdens on their revenue for welfare, education, and other services than does the United States. (Military manpower is very expensive to maintain and accounts for more than half the defense expenditures of most countries in the world.) But second, and more important, the European countries, especially Germany, have come to feel that tactical nuclear weapons are their surest form of deterrent simply because of the danger of "escalation" that they create. Europe is well aware of the increasing vulnerability of the United States, and many Europeans have come to take an exaggerated view of the extent to which American vulnerability now precludes her use of strategic weapons in response to any but an all-out attack on herself as well as Europe. But they see

* The clearest explanation of this problem is Sir Solly Zuckerman's "Control in Modern War," *Foreign Affairs*, January, 1962.

in American tactical weapons, dispersed through the NATO forces in Europe, their surest guarantee that Soviet action against their own countries would almost inescapably "trigger" American strategic action. Hence, they argue, the knowledge that this is so effectively deters the Russians from making any military move in Europe and is thus the surest safeguard of their security. Unfortunately, American suggestions for decreasing dependence on nuclear weapons in Europe and for increasing Europe's own conventional forces have been misinterpreted as the first signs of American "nuclear disengagement" from Europe, and have raised quite disproportionate fears.

This argument could be resolved if both sides were prepared to listen to the other's arguments instead of lecturing each other. The course of wisdom is, first, on the American side to recognize the real problems that confront the European powers in sustaining a high level of military manpower. Second, both parties must look more closely at the military realities of Europe, where a NATO force of some twenty-four to twenty-six divisions in West Germany with very little in the way of reinforcement behind it confronts a Soviet force of some twenty divisions with substantial reinforcement behind it. That Soviet force could not make a surprise attack without being increased, perhaps tripled, by reinforcements from Russia, a process that would take several weeks to complete and could be adequately detected. The European fear of surprise attack has few foundations (in any case, with Russia's overwhelming MRBM strength, an attack would more likely take the form of a missile strike than a ground attack). Equally, a force of twenty-six divisions could no more withstand a full-scale Soviet attack of, say, a hundred divisions without resort to nuclear weapons than one of thirty divisions or even forty or fifty.* To withdraw nuclear weapons from Europe altogether might be to invite an attempt to conquer and cripple a Western Europe of whose economic power and dynamic the Soviet Union is increasingly apprehensive.

But third, the Americans, who from their knowledge of the over-

* See Henry Kissinger, "The Unsolved Problems of European Defense," *Foreign Affairs*, July, 1962.

all strategic balance (of which they are still virtually the sole cus-
todians) have a strong apprehension of the dangers of accidental
war, have a real point in arguing that the command and control of
the nuclear weapons that are kept in Europe must be improved and
centralized if NATO is to increase rather than diminish stability
there. This the Europeans should be prepared to accept for what
it is intended to be, a policy designed to lower the risks of war
rather than, as some German writers argue, one to devalue the
deterrent.

As far as conventional forces are concerned, what this really
comes down to is an argument about quality rather than quantity.
If the Soviets are effectively deterred from a major attack on
Western Europe or its flanks, the danger of some sudden *promenade militaire* remains—a sudden grab for an exposed city like Hamburg, a landing in northern Norway, or the fomentation of civil war
in Greece. Europe is cutting its own throat if it expects the United
States to risk a thermonuclear exchange to reverse a limited thrust
of this kind, and the surest protection is to work toward making the
forces in the central area into an elite force of high mobility, discipline, experience, and firepower, rather than a large force. This is
easier said than done, for the twenty-four to twenty-six divisions
are drawn from eight nations; they are unevenly equipped; and only
the five American divisions are up to strength (by a quirk of planning, these are stationed in Bavaria, with a mountain wall on two
sides of them, farthest from the scene of potential trouble). Moreover, the question of equipment is as important as manpower. The
Soviet forces in East Germany are regularly re-equipped with the
latest weapons, while many NATO contingents are still lacking
crucial elements of mobility and firepower, such as armored person-
nel carriers or antitank missiles. One unfortunate effect of the general, and very understandable, hypnosis with nuclear weapons, in
both the United States and Europe, has been to divert effort and
resources from developing conventional weapons to their fullest
technological capabilities. This is a mistake that the Russians have
not made.

The other very difficult problem of security and stability in Europe that modern weapons have created concerns air support. The Russians can maintain almost twice as large a force of fighters and fighter bombers in Central Europe as NATO can. Therefore, to prevent the NATO forces from being at a decisive inferiority should war break out, it would be necessary to strike immediately at a large number of airfields deep in Eastern Europe, as well as at military installations and vulnerable points such as bridges, and at the Soviet communications system. In theory, that can be done with conventional bombs. But the densities of antiaircraft fire that can be concentrated around vulnerable points are now so considerable that there might be understandable reluctance to risk valuable aircraft if a conventional bomb only *might* do the job when a nuclear bomb certainly *would* do it. Consequently, the danger is that, while attempts are being made to defend Western Europe by conventional means for as long as possible on the ground, nuclear weapons would be used at the outset in the air-interdiction role. It is true that interdiction can now be performed by a variety of missiles, but, again, there is a natural reluctance to use very costly missiles except with a nuclear warhead. Thus, at present, the interdiction forces seem even more inflexibly tied to the early or first use of nuclear weapons than the ground forces.

IV

The security of Europe and the political cohesion of NATO cannot at any point be divorced from the question of the over-all strategic balance of power. It is the fact that the maintenance of this balance is effectively in the hands of one member of the Alliance that makes it so difficult to operate its consultative and policy-making organs smoothly, or to keep Europe in step with the United States.

The first edition of this book was written under the shadow of the "missile gap," when it was generally believed that by about 1962 or 1963, the Soviet Union would have a decisive superiority over the

United States in ICBM's. This mistaken perspective arose partly from faulty intelligence and special pleading of certain service authorities in Washington; and partly from a confusion of capabilities and intentions—an assumption that the Soviet Union must attempt a program of which she was industrially and technologically capable. In fact, it is now clear, as was pointed out in the previous chapter, that the Soviet Union is not attempting to match the United States missile for missile, let alone overtake it. As far as intercontinental capability is concerned, she is intent on producing a relatively small number of missiles with a very high yield. As far as Europe is concerned, she is producing a missile large enough to have both a counter-force capability—at least as far as the major NATO airfields and military installations are concerned—and a counter-city capability.

The missile gap has vanished; for in terms of units of strategic delivery (free falling bombs, ground to ground, submarine, or air-launched missiles), the United States and Britain have about 3,000 units of between 100 kilotons and 5 megatons that can be launched against the Soviet Union, whereas the Soviet Union has perhaps 300 that can be launched against the United States and perhaps 2,000 against NATO as a whole. By about 1965–66, the total of Western strategic delivery units will have risen to about 5,000. In terms of ICBM's alone, the Western advantage is now of the order of 3 to 1, and might be 8 or 10 to 1 later in the 1960's.

Thus the fears which were prevalent in the late 1950's that the strategic balance, measured in terms of numbers of planes and missiles, might tilt decisively against the West have been largely proved groundless. If there was ever a time when the Soviet Union considered a knock-out blow against American retaliatory power as a conceivable option open to her, which might have been the case in 1957 and 1958, that time has now passed. The strategic balance is now more secure than at any time since the nuclear age began.

For the time being, and unless some major technological breakthrough—such as a foolproof antimissile defense—occurs, the problem of the strategic stability of the East-West balance of power is no longer centered around the direct threats that the two super-powers pose to each other's homeland. Each has its own methods of deterring the other's direct attack. The problem of stability centers around this awkward confrontation in Europe at which we have briefly glanced in the previous section, and around an even more awkward problem which is coming to preoccupy the NATO countries more and more. This is whether the resurgence of Western Europe and its development into a single economic entity imply the rise of a new great political power in the world; whether NATO as an alliance can be refashioned in the form of a partnership of two major powers; and whether this form of interdependence can be developed without presenting to the Soviet Union a magnificent opportunity to divide one half of the Atlantic Alliance from the other.

3

EUROPE AND AMERICA:
THE CHANGING BALANCE

I

In considering the vast changes that have taken place and will continue to take place in the nature of Soviet strength, it is easy to forget that changes of equally far-reaching consequences have been taking place within the Atlantic Alliance itself. Unlike the Warsaw Pact, NATO is not a monolithic structure but a free association of sovereign states, and alterations in the relative strength of different countries have a direct bearing on the vitality and structure of the Alliance itself.

Despite the restraint with which the United States exercised its leadership ten years ago, no one could be in any doubt that NATO was an alliance that derived its security almost entirely from this one country. The gap between the productive capacity of the United States and that of the other NATO members encompassed every field of activity from nylon stockings to bomber aircraft. Hence, the commitment of the United States to Article 5 of the Treaty—that an armed attack against one signatory "shall be considered an attack against them all"—was one of the most revolutionary acts in American history. And it was a commitment to a group of eleven (now fourteen) other nations which, with the exception of the United Kingdom, possessed virtually no modern military equipment or forces of their own. Moreover, American air power, limited though it then was to a very restricted nuclear capability, represented the only hope of deterring the further erosion of Europe.

The original formula on which NATO rested—say, from 1949 to 1951—did, therefore, envisage a form of interdependence. European ground and tactical air power were to be rapidly reconstructed with American help to provide for the actual *defense* of Western Europe, while American air and sea power, based on an invulnerable North America, was held in the background as a *deterrent* to any Soviet move against Europe. Behind the protective wall thus established, the Marshall Plan was to do its beneficent work of rebuilding the war-shattered European economies, until the point was reached when they could dispense with American military aid.

This system, whereby the major ally performed a quite different function to that of the other members, broke down when the Korean War, which was interpreted as indicating the danger of a Soviet move against Europe, forced the United States to station five of its own divisions in Europe. At the same time, the necessities of deterrence forced her to embark on the development of a series of strategic air bases in England and North Africa (as well as many points outside the NATO area). The years 1951–53 were probably the most active in NATO's first decade. A case can be made for saying that at the end of 1953, when there were 15 NATO divisions in Central Europe and when 100 airfields had been built, the balance between NATO and the Soviet bloc was the most satisfactory that has ever been achieved from the Western point of view, for Russia had then no long-range striking power, and the reequipment of the Soviet ground forces had only just started. During those years, there was little talk of interdependence or specialization, for the major NATO countries were engaged in a crash rearmament program (stimulated by American aid), and all the NATO members, big and small, were feverishly trying to make up for the deficiencies of the postwar years. Moreover, from the European standpoint, the Korean War had produced a firm American commitment to the actual defense of Europe. With General Eisenhower at SHAPE and with the foundation of a NATO Secretariat, there were the makings of an integrated coalition. It looked as if the Western world was on the edge of a great advance, not so much toward a system of interdependence as toward integration and perhaps even federation.

But, unfortunately, during the years 1954, 1955, and 1956—between, that is, Mr. Dulles' speech to the Foreign Policy Association in January, 1954, with its emphasis on massive retaliation, and the Suez expedition of November, 1956—NATO stagnated as a military coalition for the defense of Europe and regressed as a political alliance. The reasons are well remembered, though it is hard at this short perspective to assign them their correct priority. One was the decision of the United States Government to base its main defensive posture on the threat of "massive retaliation at times and places of our own chosing" (an excellent analysis of the past, but no guide to the future). This was followed by talk in Washington that the NATO ground forces (or at any rate the American component of them) were mainly in Europe as a "tripwire" or "plate glass window" to provide the necessary *casus belli* for American strategic retaliation against any Soviet move in Western Europe. When, at the meeting of the NATO Council in December, 1954, this strategic concept was wedded to the decision to base tactical atomic weapons forward in Europe, it produced an acute sense of fear, notably in Germany, about the effects of becoming involved in a war between the United States and the Soviet Union—the more so since the Soviet Union, with its talk of coexistence, sometimes appeared to be more actively concerned with lowering tension than the United States. Moreover, it became harder and harder for European political leaders to understand why they should undergo the political risks of raising more military manpower, when the purpose and value of conventional forces in Europe were clearly in doubt.

Another cause of stagnation in the development of an adequate European defense system was the protracted debate on EDC, and the consequent delay in the build-up of the German forces, which meant that the first German units were not available to NATO until seven years after the initial decision of principle had been taken. A great deal of useful work went quietly on in the construction of pipelines and airfields, but much of the urgency disappeared from the planning of antiair and antisubmarine defense systems, although the extent of Soviet progress in these forms of threat was apparent at least by mid-1954.

The principal cause of political disunity during these middle years was the fact that the main points of tension were outside the NATO area—in Indochina, the Middle East, and North Africa—where the political interests of the three major NATO powers were directly involved, but where only some commercial interests of the smaller NATO powers were in jeopardy. These were the years of the formation of SEATO and the Baghdad Pact, and finally of the debacle of Suez. Over six months before Suez, a discreet mutiny on the part of the smaller NATO powers had come to a head with the decision to appoint a special committee of "three wise men" (Mr. Pearson of Canada, Mr. Lange of Norway, Mr. Martino of Italy) to consider ways of improving political consultation. The shock and heart-searching that the Suez affair caused, together with the institutional reforms in the NATO Council recommended by the three, served as an impetus to improving the quality and value of consultation within the North Atlantic Council. There is now less talk of first- and second-class membership of NATO than there was five years ago, since the larger powers, especially the U.S. and Britain, have been more scrupulous in keeping the NATO Council informed of their policies and interest in other areas. An improvement in manners is, however, no substitute for a coherent theory of interdependence.

II

Despite the effort that has recently been made to tackle NATO's problems in a more energetic way, there are a number of factors that make any coherent theory of interdependence difficult to translate into terms of political and military planning. For one thing, the demands that are now made on the resources of the United States for the defense of her own continent, coupled with the fact that she has developed an adverse balance of payments, make it impossible to assume that the expansion of the total military effort of the Alliance, which the increased flexibility of Soviet power requires, can be met by the United States alone.

The European members of NATO cannot discount the importance of North American defense, or demand that their allies across the Atlantic devote less of their resources to it. For if the credibility of the American deterrent based on North America were ever jeopardized—if, for instance, the Russians thought they could achieve 100 per cent or even 95 per cent damage to the SAC bases in the United States—then the diplomatic as well as the strategic position of the Alliance as a whole would be irreparably damaged. It is true that the European members of NATO would have a reasonable case for asking whether American priorities had been correctly thought out if an American administration were to engage in, say, a vast program of civil-defense shelters. But the development of such things as antimissile warning systems, the "hardening" of the SAC and missile bases in the United States, the fulfillment of the Polaris submarine program, and even perhaps the development of an antimissile system, are reasonable precautions which, in default of an agreement on surprise attack or disarmament, are necessary for the Alliance as a whole. And they are all formidably costly.

It is true that with the return of the Democrats to power in 1960, the preoccupation with balanced budgets and the restraint of government expenditure which marked the eight years of Republican rule gave way to a more liberal conception of American capabilities. But the domestic cost of new weapons systems has been rising sharply, and, since 1958, a new factor has entered into the problem, in that the United States has been running a serious adverse balance, primarily with Western Europe. American expenditure on troops and defense installations around the world amounts to over $3 billion in foreign exchange, of which well over $1 billion is spent in Europe. President Eisenhower had already said, in October, 1959, that the United States could no longer be looked upon as "an Atlas trying to carry the whole world," and President Kennedy has several times reiterated this warning in much sharper terms. The limitations on American power—not the power to deter war but the ability to underwrite every form of defense preparation in every corner of the globe—are nowhere more heavily stressed than in Washington. And the limitations on American capabilities might be further strained by the re-emergence of China as a significant military power.

This American sense of malaise at carrying too large a share of the Western burden needs, at least in the context of defense, a certain qualification. The United States has now taken over from the old European colonial powers most of their responsibilities in the Far East and Southeast Asia. She is not anxious to see them attempt to resume them (though she is anxious to see Britain retain a military presence in the Indian Ocean area, where she herself has no bases). It is primarily in Europe that she is anxious for a greater effort from her allies, but to get it means adjusting the whole perspective of the Alliance to a drastically changed relationship between the powers on each side of the Atlantic.

One reason why NATO often seems slow in adjusting to changes in the external world is that its member governments are naturally averse (except in the wake of a grave crisis such as Suez) to acknowledging and adjusting themselves to changes in the balance of power within the Alliance. Yet, if the outside world has changed beyond recognition in the twelve years since the North Atlantic Treaty was signed, so also have relationships between the NATO powers themselves. It seems to me that there are three trends which have been discernible for the last year or two that must be taken as fully into account as external developments, if the Alliance is to develop greater cohesion and strength and its central institution is to acquire greater authority.

The first and most important is the gradual change in the politico-strategic relation of the United States to its European

NATO allies, and vice versa. Here there seem to be on both sides two contrary forces at work. On the one hand, as the problem of maintaining a credible system of strategic deterrence in the open West becomes more and more complex, the disparity between the strategic resources of the United States and those of the European allies becomes more marked. As the deterrent forces come to center increasingly around the nuclear submarine, the "hard-based" missile, and elaborate satellite or other early-warning systems, the dependence of the Allies on the United States becomes greater, for these are projects that not only require resources no single European country or even, perhaps, the new Community collectively could command, but also are the product of continuous American programs of research and development in which European countries have only partially or fitfully engaged. Even if the European allies in concert were to decide to compete in this sphere, they could not match the geographic advantages (of increasing importance in the missile era) that a large, relatively sparsely populated land area and the proximity of two great oceans give to the United States. One cannot avoid the conclusion that the strategic pre-eminence of the United States, which was decisive even during the hegemony of the medium bomber, is likely to increase no matter what the strategic policy of Britain, France, or the other European NATO allies, and no matter what their leaders may feel or say about the impossibility of being dependent on another country for their ultimate survival.

In the short run, this may also be true of tactical forces. Because the French forces are only now, after Algeria, being reorganized into a modern army, because Britain, with an endemic balance-of-payments problem and continuing Far Eastern commitments, is a relatively weak tactical power in terms of Europe, and because the dramatic economic growth of the rest of Europe has led to an acute manpower shortage in many countries, the main burden of increasing the flexibility of Western strategy and diplomacy is likely, for the next year or two, to fall principally on the United States, which, for a number of reasons, can expand the size of her conventional forces more easily than her allies. Unless and until European defense policies are adjusted, the dominance of the United States in NATO will continue to extend to every aspect of defense planning. Moreover, American strategic forces (other than her ground forces based in Europe) will less and less depend on European bases (except for valuable but not vital facilities such as those for air refueling and submarine replenishment) when the main weight of American deterrence becomes concentrated in the Polaris submarines and on the Minutemen and B-52's based in the United States. This in turn will attenuate the already tenuous physical control over American strategic policy or decisions which some European governments have considered that they exercise by reason of having American strategic weapons based on their soil.

But in the larger political context, I think most thoughtful Americans would acknowledge that the United States, largely as a result of the external pressures we have examined, is now becoming more dependent on, and more directly affected by, the policies of her European NATO allies. For one thing, as international relations become more complex with the steady increase in the number of sovereign states, as action in one area tends to react more rapidly and forcibly on others, as Soviet and Chinese policies become increasingly concerned with discrediting the Atlantic Allies as a whole in the eyes of the uncommitted world, so the United States is increasingly affected by the colonial policies of her European allies or by their continuing relations with their former colonies. This is particularly true of developments in Africa, the dark continent on which so much light is now focused. The American attempt, in the earlier days of NATO, to stand as the champion of anticolonialism while maintaining an intimate political relationship in NATO with Britain, France, Belgium, Holland, and Portugal not only proved unconvincing to the world at large, but has less and less relevance now that the three most important colonial powers are committed to policies of "dis-imperialism." These new policies help to solve the American dilemma, but they also create new problems for the United States just as much as for her European allies.

For another, the Kennedy Administration has, as I have said, expressed a very understandable desire to shift more of the burden of upholding the free world on to the shoulders of her increasingly prosperous and dynamic allies. In its material aspect, this means greater European participation in foreign-aid and technical-assistance programs. In its military aspect, it means greater European participation in the defense of the NATO area, and greater assistance in building up the contingency reserves for possible use outside it. In its human aspect, it means giving greater weight to European experience and knowledge, particularly of former colonial areas in Asia and Africa. And in its moral aspect, it means the development of a sense of common identity between American policies and those of her leading European allies, so that the diplomatic and political onus of confronting the Soviet bloc or of representing the interests of the free world is not borne solely by the United States.

III

In the relationship of the European Allies to the United States, it seems to me that these two trends—the increasing military dominance of the United States and her increasing political, economic, and tactical dependence on Europe—can be seen in reverse. The European NATO powers, whether they are prepared to acknowledge it or not, become strategically more dependent on American technological prowess all the time. Even Britain, which once aspired to a measure of strategic independence, must seek at best a wholly interdependent relationship with the United States if her strategic deterrent system is to retain any credibility through the middle and later 1960's.* By the same token, the attempt to construct a French system of strategic deterrence around a small force

---

* This dependence was dramatically illustrated during the meeting in Nassau in December, 1962, between President Kennedy and Prime Minister Macmillan. The decision of the American Administration to abandon the Skybolt air-to-ground missile forced Britain to do likewise. The British Government will now be dependent on the supply of American Polaris missiles to maintain a deterrent system after 1967.

of manned bombers by 1965, and around an IRBM by 1970, is now widely questioned, even in French Government circles. In other words, the United States is theoretically in an even stronger position than she was in the past to direct or, if she insists, to dictate the military policy of the Alliance.

But the allies with whom the United States must maintain close political relations are very different societies from those whose governments signed the North Atlantic Treaty twelve years ago. Most of them have recovered, and far surpassed, their old economic and social dynamism: they have restored and extended their own interests and contacts throughout the world; in the European Community they have—with keen American encouragement—started to forge a powerful force for uniting and expressing Europe's interests. At the same time, their confidence in American political leadership, which was very high in the early days of NATO, is today qualified: partly because of the mistakes of the Eisenhower years; partly because of the failure of the American policy-making process in Washington to mature and develop at the same pace as the development of America's physical powers and responsibilities; partly, in the NATO and Cold War context, by reason of a less ideological and more empiric assessment of Soviet political aims and the requirements of coexistence. Indeed, the American school of thought that was in the past nervous of strengthening or extending the functions of NATO for fear of associating the United States too closely with the old colonial powers has its counterpart in the fears of many Europeans at being too closely associated with the United States in NATO lest they damage their own relations with the new or uncommitted countries.

It is obviously unwise to attempt any generalizations about an area of such diverse national psychologies and traditions of thought as Europe. What is beyond dispute, in my view, is that the restored pride and ambition of Europe make it likely that its countries will tend to play a critical or even obstructive role in the formulation of Allied policy unless a means can be found that gives them full responsibility to play an important and constructive role. Equally,

unless Europe can come to play an important part in the formulation of Allied military strategy, the temptation to develop a purely
European strategy, including a European nuclear deterrent, must
grow. Moreover, there can be no reason to assume that this is not
a permanent development or is likely to be less marked when certain grand old men of a passing generation have quit the European
scene, for the new Europe is not the creation merely of De Gaulle,
Adenauer, and Macmillan. There is no inherent reason why the
new Europe should not accept the equity and logic of the Kennedy
Administration's desire to share more of the present American burden with Europe, but only if Europe is given a larger voice in deter-
mining the policies that it necessitates. The change in the nature of
the external challenge makes it as impossible for the United States
to use her increasing strategic dominance in the Alliance to lay
down general policies for the West—which in effect she tried to do
during much of the 1950's—as it is impossible for the European
NATO Allies to develop or maintain independent credible systems
of strategic nuclear deterrence. This increasing dependence of the
two halves of the Alliance on each other could be the source of
enormous friction in the years ahead, or of a better working relationship and more powerful central institutions—depending on the
intelligence and candor with which it is faced.

IV

Another important factor in the changing balance of power
within the Alliance also springs from the recovery of Europe. The
implicit assumptions on which the institutions of NATO, certainly
the military ones, were founded was that the Alliance consisted of
three powers with world-wide interests and responsibilities—the
United States, Britain and France—and nine (later increased to
twelve) countries whose primary interest was in the security of
their own particular area. This view corresponded closely with
reality in the early 1950's, when Britain and France were still im-
perial powers in the old sense, and when the other European coun-

tries were still preoccupied with the reconstruction of their domestic economies. But the distinction is now increasingly blurred. The global responsibilities of Britain and France have diminished (though they are still of importance), and Britain is increasingly reluctant to use military means for the defense of her own without the support of allies. Moreover, the interests and influence of the other NATO countries have increased. Italy, for instance, has developed important economic, and to some extent political, relations of her own with the Middle East and Eastern Europe. Canada is expanding her relations not only throughout the Commonwealth but in the Far East. Germany plays an increasingly important part in the defense of Europe, and is spreading her interests throughout the world. Turkey is vitally involved in the affairs of the Middle East. Norway and Greece are now world-wide shipping powers. The Netherlands has an unfinished chapter in her relations with Southeast Asia. Belgium and Portugal still have vital roles to play, for good or ill, in Africa.

No doubt it is possible, on a narrow definition of overseas interests and responsibilities, to make out a case for regarding Britain and France as "world powers" still, in a sense that the others are not. The essential point, however, is that the distinction is now too tenuous to be made the basis of an effective formula for Allied cooperation and coordination of policy in the years ahead. This distinction will die hard in France, for the notion of a tripartite directorate of NATO is dear to the heart of every Frenchman, as well as to President de Gaulle. It will die hard in Britain, which still has some valid reasons for considering herself a world power in the sense that her European allies are not. But any attempt to continue the old formula will create unceasing friction between the "great," the "middle," and the "small" powers in NATO, and markedly weaken their willingness to accept the risks and strains that membership of NATO involves.

Thus, the only long-term solution is to find a way of drawing all thirteen countries into closer association with the United States, at least until such time as seven or more of them have laid the foundations of a new European superpower. For between them the thirteen allies have a range of world-wide interests, information, opportunities, and commitments equal to America's, whereas no smaller group of NATO powers has. There would be a curious irony in erecting a Franco-British-American troika in Paris at the moment when we are resisting one in Geneva and New York.

The third development in the relations between the Atlantic powers themselves may provide the incentive to develop a means of strengthening the political authority of NATO. This is the development of stronger regional associations on both sides of the Atlantic. The British Government failed in 1963 to negotiate membership in the European Economic Community, but the very strength of the French challenge makes Britain more interested in her European links. This change in British policy is likely to have certain very important effects within NATO. Quite apart from the recasting of her relationships with the Commonwealth nations on which so much attention has been focussed, it means that she is tacitly abandoning the attempt, which has dominated her postwar policy, to maintain a special relationship in political and military matters with the United States, and has accepted the force of the Kennedy Administration's contention that her influence in Washington will henceforth be commensurate with her influence in Paris, Bonn, and other capitals of Continental Europe. This altered perspective in London is likely to have a double effect. In the first place, Britain's decision to give a high priority to political and economic relations with her European neighbors, and to enter (when she can negotiate terms of entry) an association with them that is not merely consultative but involves a certain cession of sovereignty and a highly coordinated system of economic and political planning, should do much to allay fears that have long been expressed in Europe of Anglo-American domination of the Alliance; it should thus weaken the demand for tripartite leadership. Second, since Britain, of all European NATO countries, is the one least likely to be attracted to the idea of a European "Third Force," the fact that she is quietly having to relinquish her special bilateral relationship with the United States is likely to make her all the more anxious to develop and strengthen the only existing forum of multilateral transatlantic political consultation, the NATO Council. The same is also likely to be true of the smaller members of EEC, who will be equally loath to sacrifice their transatlantic links. EEC may in time acquire some useful responsibility in defense matters, even perhaps come to discharge some of the functions of the abortive EDC. One can well envisage a European defense authority to coordinate production and handle certain defense problems, such as the defense of Mediterranean or Persian Gulf oil, that are of greater concern to Europe than to the United States. But the smaller powers will be unhappy if such a development means precluding the direct contact of European governments with the source of virtually all Western strategic power, the United States. The political and military development of EEC is therefore dependent upon the strengthening of NATO.

If one is right in thinking that these six developments—the widening of the Soviet challenge to the West as a consequence of nuclear parity, the growing difficulty of maintaining a stable system of international relations in the age of "dis-imperialism," the importance of civil control over military decision and of unified diplomatic action, the increasing military dependence of Europe on the United States and the growing political dependence of the United States on Europe, the blurring of the old distinction in NATO between powers of greater and lesser interests, and the needs and desire to offset the trend toward regionalism within the Alliance—are those that are likely to have the most far-reaching effects upon security and cohesion, then certain conclusions seem to me to follow. The first is that the significance and authority of the political institutions of the Alliance must be enhanced. Related to this is the need to develop entirely new means of interposing political judgment between every step of military planning, whether long-term or emergency. Both problems require an Allied solution since a closer working arrangement on political questions merely between the larger powers in NATO no longer meets the needs of the case.

The second is that the defense of Europe, which will remain the central responsibility of NATO, needs reconsideration, in the light not merely of the Berlin crisis, but of changes in the strategic and technological environment.

v

No discussion of the changing balance of power within the Alliance can be complete without some exploration of the growing divergence that has developed between Washington and the European capitals over the whole concept of European and Atlantic security, for its resolution is fundamental to the continuation of NATO as an effective instrument of policy.

Broadly, it is a fact that the United States has not only become very much more powerful as a nuclear power—absolutely, and probably in relation to the Soviet Union—but has also become increasingly aware of the danger that a nuclear war might start by accident or by some other hand than her own, especially in Europe, where the two blocs confront each other with such a high level of armaments on both sides. This has had two effects on American policy, as exemplified by the actions and statements of the Kennedy Administration during the Berlin crisis of 1961–62. On the one hand, it has increased the American desire to create a more flexible defense system in Central Europe, most particularly one that makes the forward troops less dependent on the early use of nuclear weapons in the case of a limited or probing attack from the East. On the other hand, it has made the United States anxious to keep a channel of communication open to the Soviet Union in periods of high tension so that misunderstandings that might lead to nuclear war can be avoided, and even to make it possible to consider removing some of the causes of friction, for instance in Berlin, that give an excuse for Soviet threats. This general approach of the United States was well exemplified in the summer of 1961 during the Berlin crisis, when the United States made virtually no nuclear threats in response to Soviet blustering, but moved two army divisions from the United States to Europe. A little later, American and Soviet diplomatic representatives embarked on exploratory conversations on the Berlin question, which, though they then proved abortive, could be resumed at any time.

In Britain, opinion and official policy have on the whole supported this general American approach, though the fact that Britain has, for better or worse, reoriented her defense policy to emphasize nuclear firepower rather than conventional manpower has made it difficult for her to give practical support to this American policy of introducing an element of flexibility into the defense of Europe. In 1961, for instance, she did not move her strategic reserve (which is only two brigades) from England to the Continent, despite American urging.

In practical terms, the British reaction to new American policy may be somewhat negative. But in France and Germany, it is almost hostile. The French attitude to the defense of Europe rests on the firm belief that war in Europe is most unlikely, and is almost inconceivable if a strong system of nuclear deterrence is maintained there. The American preoccupation with the danger of nuclear war tends to be dismissed as neurotic, and the American desire to keep open a channel of communication to the Soviets as unwise and unnecessary. The policy of the Kennedy Administration has tended to strengthen the French conviction that the United States is increasingly preoccupied with the vulnerability of its own cities; that the American desire to create a more flexible defense system in Europe means, in effect, that the United States is less and less ready to go to war for Europe; and that the case for having a European system of strategic deterrence free from American control is getting stronger with each passing year. The American contention—so graphically expressed by Secretary of Defense McNamara in his speech at Ann Arbor on June 16, 1962—that the United States has adequate nuclear retaliatory power to protect her allies, and that she alone has this power, has been greeted in France with considerable skepticism.

In Germany, the reaction has been somewhat different. Many Germans would agree with their French counterparts that the American policy suggests that the stakes for which the United States is prepared to risk war in Europe are rising as the United States becomes more vulnerable. But where France may regard this as inevitable, and indeed not wholly undesirable—since it gives Western Europe greater freedom of diplomatic maneuver—Germany is mainly afraid of such a development. Many of the American attempts to reduce overdependence on nuclear weapons in Europe have been misinterpreted in Germany as the thin end of the wedge of American disengagement from the Continent. If the British and the Americans fear the danger of "escalation" from a minor incident to general war, Germans regard this danger as one of their greatest safeguards, arguing that this same fear must inhibit the Russians not only from general aggression in Europe but from some limited *coup de main* against the all-too-small real estate of West Germany. Hence the firm opposition of the West German Government to the reduction of tactical nuclear weapons in Germany.

The Alliance cannot face the tests of the future unless this confusion of motives and perspectives among its four principal members can be reduced to a more orderly pattern of agreed policy.

4

THE IDEA OF INTERDEPENDENCE

"Interdependence" is a word that has only recently gained international currency. The word, and to a lesser extent the idea itself, derives from the conversation that was held between the British Prime Minister, Mr. Harold Macmillan, and President Eisenhower in Washington in October, 1957, when the clouds of Anglo-American discord over Suez had been dissipated, but when Sputnik had added a new urgency to the strengthening of NATO. In the words of their communiqué:

> The arrangements which the nations of the free world have made for collective defense and mutual help are based on the recognition that the concept of national self-sufficiency is out of date. The countries of the free world are interdependent, and only in genuine partnership, by combining their resources and sharing tasks in many fields, can progress and safety be found. For our part, we have agreed that our two countries will henceforth act in accordance with this principle.

It can be argued that the fundamental principle on which NATO has always operated is that of interdependence in the sense that it was used in this quotation. But it can hardly be said that the affairs of the Alliance have been conducted in constant recognition of it. As far as the coordination of policy was concerned, the tacit American reservation in joining NATO was that the United States would retain its freedom of action in the Pacific, just as Britain in those early years intended to retain her full freedom of action in the Middle East and France in Southeast Asia. During the middle years, all three powers were anxious to remind their fellow members that NATO was only one of several treaty obligations which they had entered into, that as far as they were concerned it was just another alliance. But the world proved too small and the overriding importance of Europe too great for such a dual attitude. The change that has taken place in recent years can be gauged from a speech made by the late Mr. Dulles at Boston in September, 1958, in which he said: "It is coming more and more to be realized that independence, which each of our nations rightly cherishes, can only be preserved by the practice of interdependence." He went on to make it plain that the United States now recognized an obligation (which Mr. Dulles himself would have carefully rejected three years earlier) to consult her NATO Allies on her Middle and Far Eastern policies, although without accepting any veto on her action or any enlargement of the NATO Treaty area.

This change in the British and American attitude toward NATO has been very marked. But even so, there has been little attempt to explore what the concept of interdependence really involves, what effect it should have upon the policies of the various countries that compose the Alliance, or what its relation is to the developing flexibility of Soviet power. Given the circumstances in which the word itself was first given prominence, it is not particularly surprising that European opinion tended for some years to regard the idea as a polite synonym for an Anglo-American dictatorship of the Alliance.

What interdependence has come to mean, at least to those who live at the heart of the Alliance, is this: that no NATO country, including the United States, is now capable of assuring its own security; in other words, that there is no longer such a thing as a national strategy even for the strongest powers in NATO, even though there may be many shades of difference in their foreign policies.

Nor can they divide their policies into compartments, pursuing an Allied strategy in Europe and a national policy elsewhere. The flexibility of Soviet power has now made a dual attitude of this kind impossible.

It may be asked why such severe limitations should have come to hedge the independence of the leading NATO powers, even the United States, when it still appears possible for Russia to pursue a wholly national strategy. Part of the answer is that Soviet independence is much more apparent than real. Russia is clearly struggling to achieve a form of interdependence with China that will impose some obligations on the latter to consult Moscow in advance of action. Moreover, she must take some account of opinion in the satellite countries: She will not willingly risk another East German or Hungarian uprising. The only truly independent powers are the neutrals. But in so far as Russia is genuinely capable of pursuing a more independent policy than the United States, it is because she is far less dependent on overseas trade and good will, because she can bring political pressure to bear at many points of the compass without using the territory or communications of any other country and, above all, because she has been prepared to sacrifice living standards to defense.

But the reasons why the Western Alliance must evolve a higher degree of interdependence than its Eastern counterpart go deeper than geography and trade. The expansion of Soviet military strength requires both a larger total effort—military, technological, and economic—in order to maintain a stable balance of power at all levels, and a greater degree of specialization among the different members of NATO. For only by differentiation of function can the superiority of the Soviet Union in many fields be adequately countered and the inevitable wastefulness inherent in any alliance be overcome. Moreover, a division of labor among the different members of the Alliance is rendered essential by the steadily rising cost and complexity of weapons.

It is important to be clear on one point. The loss of independence of action is not the same thing as an abrogation of sovereignty. The proof demonstrated by various events from Suez to Cuba, that the NATO powers must draw closer together has produced much heart-searching among thoughtful people and a revival of interest in an Atlantic federation. Most people would agree that such a federation is politically impossible and would be a dubious gain in strength and flexibility if it were possible. It is a forlorn hope, because a federation of democracies requires a legislature that is directly elected by the peoples of the federated area. This may be possible within the European community of seven or nine nations by the end of the next decade, though even this is not certain. It could not happen on an Atlantic scale within our lifetime, most particularly because the United States is now a world power whereas her allies are not. Moreover, it would be a dubious step because an international government might be considerably less efficient and flexible —particularly at the administrative level—than a number of national governments working on an agreed plan. An analogy with the founding of the United States of America is misleading in this respect, because it was founded at a time when central governments had minuscule responsibilities by comparison with today.

What emerges from any attempt to apply the concept of interdependence to the next ten years of NATO is not a blueprint for new institutions (although the extent to which the present ones are adequate to the task ahead of them will be considered later) but guiding principles in three major areas of policy.

II

The growing diffusion of economic power among the Allies implies a greater, not a lesser, obligation on the NATO powers to consult in advance of action on problems affecting not only the NATO area but the whole world. As the world grows smaller, so any ideas of spheres of influence become less tenable, even though it may become no easier for an Italian or Belgian minister to see the problems of the North Pacific through American eyes, or for an American or Danish official to see African problems through

French or British eyes. If one danger of war lies in the possible expansion of a local conflict into a limited war, and from a limited war upward, a fracas in Laos or Quemoy or Nairobi is something that affects countries far from the scene of action. In this sense, General de Gaulle's request to Washington in October, 1958, for a general review of the world situation on the part of the United States, France, and Britain was a legitimate one—though his refusal to participate in many vital aspects of European defense unless France were given access to, and a virtual veto on, American action anywhere in the world was not.

There has been one development in recent years that has led to a marked improvement in the use of the NATO Council as an instrument of political consultation. This is the virtual end of European colonialism. Nothing impaired the value of NATO as a political instrument more than the fact that, on the one hand, the United States was a close ally of European powers in Europe but either hostile or unsympathetic to their problems in Asia and Africa, and, on the other, that the colonial powers could not discuss their colonial problems with the other allies. Except for the unhappy remnants of Portuguese colonialism in Africa, this source of friction is now largely removed, and instead the emergent states of the postcolonial world, most particularly those in Africa, confront all the NATO powers, including the United States, with common problems of internal stability, aid, or investment. The consequence is that the larger powers can make much greater use of the consultative machinery of NATO than was the case a few years ago.

It is the very fact that most of the NATO powers have wide and various interests outside the Alliance that makes this principle of consultation in advance of action so important. It would be a source of weakness rather than of strength if NATO were to become a monolithic bloc whose members were always expected to act in exact concert at the U.N., in Africa, or in Asia, or to create some "Cold War general staff," as has been suggested. It is the breadth and diversity of Western contacts with the rest of the world that gives the Atlantic Community much of its moral and political strength. But so interwoven have all forms of initiative and reaction become, especially in the military field, that the only alternative to an insistence that no action be taken by any member anywhere in the world without the unanimous agreement of, say, the NATO Council (an arrangement that might break up the Alliance) is to insist on the principle of regular though informal consultation in advance of action.

To this rule there must, for the foreseeable future, be one exception. In the unlikely, but conceivable, event of a Soviet surprise attack or threat against Europe or the United States or both, mounted without any warning, the President of the United States would default in his obligation to the Allies if he did not take immediate action even if it meant no consultation whatever.* Of this the Russians must be in no doubt.

Closely linked with the principle of consultation is that of negotiation. It has become fashionable to suggest that the United States and Russia would make greater headway in negotiations on nuclear tests, disengagement, or disarmament if they could talk *tête-à-tête* without being "compassed about with so great a cloud of witnesses" in the shape of their smaller allies. Much of the European nervousness at the prospect of summit conferences has derived from a fear that both Moscow and Washington may believe this to be true, though there is no evidence to show that it is.

But true or not, such an approach cannot be reconciled with the idea of interdependence within NATO. This may prove to be a drawback, but it cannot be avoided. NATO is by no means an ideal alliance: it is very far from being "one equal temper of heroic hearts"; it comprises states of very different historical backgrounds, of very unequal levels of wealth, skill, and wisdom. But for better or worse, it is the only transatlantic alliance that has ever been created in time of peace, and it is at present the most effective that can be achieved. Therefore, the larger powers within it cannot at

---

* In my view, President Kennedy's decision to impose a blockade around Cuba on October 23, 1962, after informing but without consulting the NATO Allies, was justified by the need to take swift action.

one moment accept the benefits it brings them and at another disregard it in order to talk with Moscow the more sophisticated dialect common to great powers. The point is that the strength of the larger powers in NATO at the conference table is directly related to the degree of fundamental agreement that exists within the Alliance as a whole.

III

NATO, it needs to be said again, is not a supranational organization. The NATO Council is really a permanent conference of ambassadors (or of foreign ministers, when it meets at that level twice a year). It does not reach decision by majority vote (like the Council of Ministers of the European Economic Community), nor are the decisions necessarily binding on governments. By the same token, the constitutent countries have not made any formal cessions of sovereignty to NATO, in either the political or the military field. In the latter they have agreed that in the event of war their forces would immediately come within an international system of command (whose framework—for instance, Supreme Headquarters and its subordinate commands in Europe—exists fullblown in peacetime) but that they would remain national forces.

Consequently, there is no question of SHAPE or any other body laying down a military strategy for the Alliance (though the commanding personalities of Generals Gruenther and Norstad, together with the dominance of the United States in the Alliance, until quite recently made it sometimes appear that SHAPE possessed such authority). The evolution of strategic policy has to emerge from constant intergovernmental negotiation and agreement, and this calls for a special approach.

Such an approach is a very difficult one for any minister or official brought up in the days when it was possible for a government to evolve a policy around its own conception of its national interest. It is one thing to make speeches about the importance for the NATO countries of subordinating individual national interests to the general interest of the Alliance. It is quite another to translate this into terms of tanks, fighters, and aircraft carriers. It is harder in military planning than in, say, economic cooperation, for there is a traditional connection that goes back many centuries to the dawn of the nation-state—and is as strong in republics as in monarchies—between military power and the pride or self-esteem of the nation itself.

But the important point, given the fact that the total military resources that are available in NATO are limited in relation to the flexibility of Soviet power and to the vast area which the Alliance covers, is that a country's influence within the Alliance must be closely related to the extent to which its military power conforms to the over-all needs of the Alliance. If it were carried to its logical conclusion, the argument used, first in Britain and then in France, that it is necessary to have a complete array of military power in order to be influential in the Standing Group or in the Council could conceivably produce six or eight separate nuclear-weapons programs within the Alliance, some of dubious military value, all overlapping, and all of great political danger. Nor is it merely a question of nuclear weapons. It is an open question whether the navies of the smaller NATO powers serve a purpose commensurate with their cost. A more effective specialization of functions is not merely a matter of getting a more objective approach by ministers and chiefs of staff when they negotiate changes in force requirements in the Council or in the Standing Group, nor is it simply a matter of attaching greater weight to the recommendations put forward there. It is also a matter of political leaders educating their own public to an understanding of what collective, as opposed to national, defense involves.

The corollary to this is that there must be a far more intensive system of consultation, and a much more profound level of agreement, about the needs of the future among the NATO powers. Twice-yearly meetings of foreign ministers and chiefs of staff and one SHAPE exercise a year are not adequate for this purpose. Too often, a glowing communiqué at the ministerial level conceals a complete lack of agreement among officials at the levels of government where NATO decisions must be translated into terms of national policy. This is important because, unlike the Anglo-American alliance of World War II, NATO is not based on a personal concordat between powerful heads of government, but depends for its effectiveness on cooperation at the working level of officialdom, civil and military. The crucial questions of future priorities, of the balances between nuclear and conventional forces and between the needs of deterrence and the likelihood of limited war, of problems of subversion and other "ambiguous" threats would seem to require a major and continuous review by both ministers and officials, rather than a series of *ad hoc* national debates of the kind that have taken place sporadically in the United States, Britain, Germany, and Canada during recent years. NATO's great failure to date is that it has not created an effective international staff, within either its civil or its military organs, to make such a continuous internal debate fruitful or constructive.

One difficulty has always been the limitations on the power of the United States Government—imposed and required by American legislation—to discuss with her allies strategic concepts, let alone national plans, that involve the use of nuclear weapons. In practice, this meant that during much of the recent past it was difficult for American representatives to discuss or explain the problems of maintaining an effective policy of nuclear deterrence, and, in consequence, the ideas of some European governments were woefully out of date. (For instance, until the beginning of 1962, the German Government had no inkling of how many or what kind of nuclear weapons were on German soil.) Britain has been the only country to whose representatives American officials can talk with full candor, a fact of which France is fully aware.

Seeing the restrictive aspect of the MacMahon Act only as it affects themselves, America's allies have sometimes failed to appreciate that one of the motives behind it was to prevent the spread of nuclear-weapons capabilities to all countries—friendly as well as unfriendly, for the Nth Power problem was acknowledged as a potential danger a decade and more ago. Now that the knowledge of how to make nuclear weapons has spread throughout the world, it is clear that the U.S. Government realizes the extent to which the Act is either a direct incentive to smaller powers to develop their own nuclear-weapons industries or a source of confusion to their policies. The establishment of the nuclear committee of the NATO Council in the spring of 1962, to which the United States and Britain promised to submit their nuclear strategic plans, is thus a development of real significance. But a great deal more is needed to make up for the shortsighted views that prevailed in Washington throughout most of NATO's first decade—in the Congress, in the Pentagon, and in the Atomic Energy Commission.

IV

It has always been easy to draw up a theoretical scheme for a more rational and intelligent division of effort on manpower and production within NATO than exists today. On a purely financial calculation, it is absurd for the United States and Canada to maintain forces of their present size in Europe; for example, the Canadian brigade in Westphalia costs as much to maintain as two European divisions. The additional manpower for the defense of Europe more rationally might be drawn from those nations where there is still underemployment. Similarly, naval construction for the Alliance should be concentrated in European yards, where ships can be built more efficiently and cheaply than in the United States. On the other hand, the production of missiles and electronic equipment could ideally be concentrated in North America, where the size of the industries concerned makes for flexibility and speed of production.

But it is unrealistic to proceed too far with arguments of this kind, for one knows that they have no chance of being implemented. The United States cannot entirely abandon the ground defense of Europe to the Europeans, because ordinary people throughout Europe would take this as a sure sign of her effective withdrawal from the Alliance. Equally important is the fact that defense production and military research are intimately interrelated with over-all national economic policies and with the nonmilitary application of scientific advances. The electronics industry is probably the best example of military-nonmilitary cross-fertilization and cross-stimulation. Moreover, the difficulty of reconciling national interests in the field of defense production becomes greater the higher the proportion of the national resources that is spent on it. With defense expenditures absorbing anywhere from a quarter to more than half of national budgets, defense production has become inextricably involved with commercial and employment policies, and the problem becomes more acute every year, as the cost and complexity of major weapons systems rise sharply.

Nevertheless, a better rationalization of effort there must be if NATO is to meet the requirements of the next decade without the imposition of heavy new burdens on the public—burdens which, even if it were politically possible to meet them, would in themselves aggravate international tension. The recent difficulty that arose over the American balance of payments may in this respect prove a blessing in disguise, for it must force NATO to take a much closer look at the unevenness of the present distribution of effort and resources. Equally, the development of the European Common Market is forcing an internal rationalization of European industry which is already having an effect in the weapons field.

The problems of economic and technical interdependence will be discussed in a later chapter. It is necessary only to make two points here. The first is to suggest that there is one formula for interdependence that certainly will not work. This is to expect Europe to concentrate on conventional forces and simple weapons while the more advanced weapons are manufactured in the United States. There is far too much pride, ambition, and enterprise in Europe to accept any such formula. But second, governments can no longer regard military production in the terms of self-sufficiency with which they look on other forms of economic activity.

II
THE
IMPLICATIONS OF
INTERDEPENDENCE

5

INTERDEPENDENCE AND NUCLEAR WEAPONS

I

The question of the control, ownership, and deployment of nuclear weapons is one of the central problems that the Alliance must solve within the next few years if it is not to regress as a center for the creation and expression of Western solidarity and political coherence. This is so for a number of reasons. The most obvious and the most cogent is that the great preponderance of Allied military strength lies in the nuclear weapons that a few of its members, primarily the United States, possess. Consequently, the influence that the nuclear powers within NATO can exert is, however tactfully exercised, very large indeed. NATO strategy, measured in terms of firepower, is overwhelmingly a nuclear strategy and is likely to remain so. But with the regeneration of economic strength and political confidence among the nonnuclear powers in NATO, they are no longer prepared to leave the formulation of such a large area of military policy to the two or three nuclear powers, especially as any miscalculation on the part of the latter would be catastrophic for them all.

Another reason why the question of the control of nuclear weapons has come to dominate inter-Allied discussion is that, with the rise of a very strong Soviet nuclear striking force, the simple guarantee of nuclear retaliation in the event of aggression, which the United States was able to offer NATO in the earlier days of the Alliance, now needs some qualification. It is not true, as some European experts have alleged, that the United States is less ready now than it was five or ten years ago to use nuclear weapons in response to major aggression in Europe, even though the cost in terms of damage to the continental United States itself has risen sharply. Both American attitudes and American policy belie any such charge. What is true is that the United States has to exercise greater caution and precision about the kinds of circumstances that would justify the use of nuclear weapons, and therefore feels obliged to make clear that any concept of automatic nuclear retaliation to a Soviet *démarche* of any kind is ruled out. This in turn means that the President must exercise the very closest control over American nuclear weapons, whether based in Europe or elsewhere. Thus, the increasing delicacy of the nuclear balance of power makes the United States anxious to tighten its grip on the nuclear strategy of NATO at a time when politically her allies are no longer fully prepared to accept such close control.

Still another reason lies in the diversification of types of nuclear weapons and the steady increase in the numbers of them in Europe. We shall have to examine the special problems to which this gives rise in the next chapter. Here it is sufficient to note that it is not merely the problem of the control of nuclear strategy that is a source of inter-Allied friction; for many countries the concern is with the control of tactical nuclear weapons.

Finally, there is the difficult relation of stability and confidence within NATO to stability in the relationship between NATO and the Soviet Union. If nuclear weapons were like other weapons, much of the inter-allied tension to which they give rise could be solved, either by encouraging the smaller allies to develop their own or by distributing American weapons outright. But whatever arguments this might settle within NATO, it would create such apprehension on the Soviet side as to weaken the over-all position of the Alliance and increase the dangers of war out of all proportion.

The first question to be considered is whether the Allies will accept a continuing American hegemony in nuclear weapons and in the formulation of nuclear strategy. The second is what real value the British and French nuclear-weapons programs now have. The third concerns the desirability of creating a European nuclear deterrent as the European Community gathers strength and cohesion. Then we must consider the suggestions that have been put forward for a NATO deterrent. And finally, we must ask whether, in view of the shortcomings of all these programs or proposals, a better compromise can be envisaged, in terms of interdependence, Allied cohesion, and Soviet reassurance, than the existing situation.

II. THE AMERICAN DETERRENT

Compared with the situation even a year or two ago, the American system of nuclear deterrence is very formidable indeed, and will become even more so during the next three or four years. It comprises at least seven different weapons systems:

1) 630 intercontinental B-52 bombers operating from North American bases.

2) An older force of medium bombers, the B-47's, operating from overseas bases, which has now been decreased from some 1,200 to 850 aircraft and 90 supersonic B-58's.

3) Some 800 naval attack aircraft with nuclear capability, operating from carrier fleets in the Pacific, Atlantic, and Mediterranean.

4) 9 nuclear submarines with 144 Polaris A-1 or -2 ballistic missiles with a range of 1,300–1,700 miles. By about 1966, this fleet will consist of 41 such submarines with a total of 650 missiles (half of which will have a 2,500-mile range).

5) About 100 Atlas liquid-fuel missiles with a range of 9,000 miles and a warhead of 3 megatons. This was the first of the American ICBM's and has many military drawbacks, in that it is vulnerable to attack and slow going into action. It is nevertheless a very formidable weapons system.

6) About 70 Titan liquid-fuel missiles with a range of 9,000 miles and a warhead of 4 megatons. About half of these are in "hardened" silos. Again this system has drawbacks but is nevertheless formidable.

7) 150 solid-fuel Minuteman missiles, out of an eventual total of 800, to be deployed in "hard" sites throughout the American mountain states. By the spring of 1963, about 500 American ICBM's will be deployed.

At the beginning of 1963, the United States will have something on the order of 3,000 delivery units for nuclear bombs or warheads with a strategic range. By about 1965–66, the figure will, unless the plans are altered, be nearer 5,000. By comparison, the Soviet Union will have, at the beginning of 1963, about 75 ICBM's capable of reaching the United States, and some 200 bombers, although it will be able to pose a threat of about 1,000 bombers and 700 medium-range missiles to areas close to it—Japan or Western Europe.

The American strategic deterrent has by now largely fulfilled the requirements of those strategic experts who, in the mid-1950's foresaw how rigorous would be the requirements of the 1960's.* The various missile programs are now sufficiently well advanced to assure a reasonable degree of dependability for the ground as well as the aircraft systems. The existence of the Polaris fleet and the beginnings of the Minuteman program, together with the various air-alert systems used for SAC, give reasonable assurance that all the systems could not be crippled by surprise attack. Although Soviet air defenses are getting stronger all the time, the development of the air-to-ground missile gives the bombers as well as the missiles adequate penetration. And it has proved possible to develop and maintain this vast complex at a bearable, even though very large, cost.

The rate of technological advance does, of course, leave a series of permanent question marks suspended above any such judgments.

* The classic statement of these requirements is in Albert Wohlstetter, "The Delicate Balance of Terror," *Foreign Affairs*, January, 1959.

It is conceivable that the Soviets are making as much progress as they claim in the development of antimissile defenses, which might have an important bearing on the effectiveness of the American systems, at least in the 1970's. If efficient and controllable means of putting mass-destruction weapons in space were embarked on, the whole nature of the strategic balance might be altered. Major advances in antisubmarine detection or submarine weapons might invalidate the Polaris or carrier-borne aircraft systems. All that one can say with reasonable assurance is that for most of the 1960's, the American deterrent system would be catastrophically effective if even part of it were ever committed to action.

But the question that has loomed large in European minds in recent years relates not so much to the system's effectiveness as to the conditions under which it would be used. For one thing, Europeans see the American strategic weapons, some of which in the 1950's were based on their own soil, being relocated, as their range increases, on American soil. Thus, they feel that they have less direct control over American strategy than they used to. For another, they know that American cities are becoming more vulnerable all the time as the megatonnage of the Soviet strategic force, which is more and more geared to a terror strategy, increases. They have seen the demise of the old American strategy of "massive retaliation" as a threat against any form of Soviet aggression, and until recently, they saw nothing very coherent to replace it.

However, in the two years since the Kennedy Administration took office, there has been an intensive effort to develop a new American strategy, suited to the needs of the Allies and designed to extract the full psychological advantage out of this multiplicity of deterrent systems. This has been the doctrine of controlled nuclear response which Mr. McNamara has outlined on several occasions, notably in his speech at Ann Arbor. Essentially, it means that if either the United States or Europe were subject to nuclear attack (or even, in the case of Europe, to massive conventional attack), the United States would first strike at Soviet bases and military installations, keeping a large force in reserve as a threat against Soviet cities. At every point during a closely controlled increase in destruction of her military potential, the Soviet Union would be faced with the alternative of suing for peace or bringing the total destruction of her own civilization a step nearer.

In this study, we are not concerned with whether such a strategy is feasible or psychologically plausible—a subject on which considerable debate will continue for some time. What concerns us here is its bearing on interdependence within the Alliance. The new American strategy has, as one of its specific purposes, to make clear to other NATO countries not only that the United States can exercise an effective system on their behalf, but that they cannot do it themselves. Mr. McNamara made a specific reference to small national deterrent forces as "dangerous, expensive, prone to obsolescence and lacking in credibility," a remark he later made clear applied directly to France.

The new American doctrine could answer certain European questions. If the United States could really prove that she can exercise an effective counter-force capability that would have the effect of minimizing damage to Europe in the event of a nuclear exchange, it would improve European confidence in the American deterrent. The difficulty is that it requires increasingly strong and self-assertive countries to leave life-and-death decisions to the President of the United States even more than they have had to do in the past. To that extent, American counter-force capability does not eliminate the pressure for either multilateral ownership or multilateral control of nuclear weapons.

III. The British Nuclear Force

The doubts that have accumulated about the present and future value of the independent British nuclear deterrent spring from several sources: from moral protests at the possession of so inhuman a weapon; from uneasiness about its effect on the policy of other NATO countries; and from misgivings as to whether it represents a right ordering of priorities in British defense planning and expenditure. The moral protests cannot be put aside as extraneous to the problem. The fact that they are heard more strongly in Britain than in other countries is not necessarily a sign of an irresolute attitude on Britain's part toward either NATO or Russia. It is closely linked with the questions that must be asked here, namely: (a) what value will British nuclear weapons have in furtherance of British security during the next ten years; and (b) given Britain's endorsement of the concept of interdependence, what value will they have for NATO as a whole?

The reasons that impelled the Labour Government of 1945–51 to embark on an independent program for the development of atomic weapons in the years immediately after World War II were valid enough. One was undoubtedly national pride. British scientists had made an important contribution to the Manhattan Project, and a great deal of expert and detailed knowledge about nuclear physics existed in Britain. But before NATO was even launched, the Fuchs and Pontecorvo cases seemed to kill for the foreseeable future any hope that the United States would make atomic weapons available to the United Kingdom or even permit a fruitful exchange of information. Responsible politicians and civil servants could not but feel that an independent capability would greatly strengthen Britain's general influence with the United States, both in peacetime planning and in the direction of any potential war.

These considerations were later strengthened by potent economic arguments. When the Korean War broke out, it was clear that to carry out the £4.7 billion conventional rearmament program to which the government had committed itself would impose such a heavy strain on the British engineering industry (one of the chief earners of a very limited supply of foreign exchange) as to invite a severe balance-of-payments crisis and thus to make it conceivable that Britain might have to abandon *any* contribution to the defense of Europe. This line of reasoning was reinforced when it became clear that the Continental members of NATO were not going to live up to their post-Korean War rearmament programs, thus at one and the same time strengthening their economic posi-

tion and jeopardizing the forward strategy of NATO. When the
Conservative Government came to review the situation in 1952–53,
Britain had exploded her first A-bomb, and had an effective means
of delivery—the V-bomber force—under development. And as an
additional reason, or rationale, it was argued that with the increase
of Soviet air and nuclear strength SAC could no longer be expected
to give the same priority in war to Soviet targets directly threaten-
ing Britain that a purely British force would. In those days before
the development of Soviet striking power had become apparent, it
was possible to conceive of British and American air power as a
means of actually defending the West.

The 1955 White Paper, which announced that Britain would
produce megaton weapons, carried this argument a stage further in
declaring that since there could now be no defense of Britain, the
only policy that ensured security was one of deterrence: "The
knowledge that aggression will be met by overwhelming nuclear
retaliation is the surest guarantee that it will not take place." Sub-
sequent statements have all been based on the same premise—that
nuclear war cannot be won, but can only be deterred. A very heavy
emphasis has always been placed in British Government statements
on the deterrent value of the British nuclear-weapons program.

There can be little doubt that the widespread feeling throughout
the country, engendered by Suez, that Britain's position as a world
power was in jeopardy played a significant part in the further increase of emphasis on the British nuclear deterrent which was made
clear in the famous White Paper of 1957 and its successor of 1958.
In 1957: "The free world is today mainly dependent for its protection upon the nuclear capacity of the United States. While Britain
cannot by comparison make more than a modest contribution,
there is a wide measure of agreement that she must possess an
appreciable element of nuclear deterrent power of her own." In
1958: "Britain's nuclear power cannot, of course, be compared in
magnitude with that of the United States. Nevertheless, when
fully equipped with megaton weapons, the British bomber force
will in itself constitute a formidable deterrent." In 1960, govern-

ment statements referred to the British program not as an "independent deterrent" but as "an independent contribution to the Western deterrent." Yet in 1962, the determination to maintain a British nuclear capability in some form was as strong as ever.

Do the considerations that prompted successive British governments to produce their own nuclear weapons and means of delivery still hold good? The first point to be noted is that the main premises on which the British nuclear-weapons program were based have altered beyond recognition. One was that the United States might assume less responsibility for Europe as a whole as its own ICBM program took shape. On April 16, 1957, Mr. Sandys said in the House of Commons: "So long as large American forces remain in Europe, and American bombers are based in Britain, it might conceivably be thought safe—I am not saying it would—to leave to the United States the sole responsibility for providing the nuclear deterrent. But when they have developed the 5,000-mile intercontinental ballistic rocket, can we really be sure that every American administration will go on looking at things in quite the same way?"* But two years later, he stated on a similar occasion: "'The point in question is whether, if the attack were made not on the United States but on one of her NATO allies in Europe, the Americans would react in the same uncompromising manner [as to an attack on themselves]. We have absolutely no doubts on this score. . . . The United States has given categorical assurances that she will regard an attack upon any NATO country as an attack upon herself, and will come to its aid with all necessary force. Her Majesty's Government place complete reliance upon this solemn understanding."†

The second premise was that it would take many years for Britain to achieve once again a position of intimacy with the United States on questions of nuclear weapons and the complex of knowledge that surrounds their manufacture and potential use. This was proved unfounded by the amendment of 1958 to the MacMahon

* Hansard, April 16, 1957, cols. 1760–61.
† Hansard, February 26, 1959, col. 1418.

Act, since which there has been a continuous exchange of information.

The third was that Britain's Continental NATO Allies would accept an increase in her nuclear deterrent power as a substitute for what she had subtracted from her contribution to the conventional defenses of Europe. This did not prove to be the case, the more so as Bomber Command remained outside the control of NATO until 1963.

But the premise of the original calculation that has been most drastically upset concerns the feasibility of Britain's maintaining a credible and effective strategic delivery system for its nuclear weapons over the next decade. In 1960, Britain's own IRBM program, Bluestreak, was canceled because the upward spiral of costs that it involved far outstripped its real value. The advent of the air-to-ground missile—the American 1,000-mile Skybolt—could have saved the V-bomber force until the useful operational life of its 180 aircraft began to draw to a close between 1968 and 1970. Thereafter, the British Government would have had only two tactical aircraft under development for nuclear weapons, the carrier-borne Buccaneer and the supersonic low-level TSR2—fine aircraft, but not capable of exercising a major strategic threat to the Soviet Union.

There is also the problem of the vulnerability of a force based in a country the size of the United Kingdom. When it was decided to base the British deterrent on the V-bomber force, it was also decided to concentrate that force primarily in the United Kingdom, rather than disperse it around the perimeter of Russia (on the analogy of SAC), partly for reasons of range, partly for sound political reasons which have become stronger ever since. The only exception to this policy has been Cyprus, where a base has been considered essential to fulfill Britain's commitments to CENTO (the Baghdad Pact). Thus, the V-bomber force is based on a group of airfields in the United Kingdom, not very far distant from each other and all of them vulnerable to megaton weapons.

It is for these reasons that Britain responded with alacrity to the American offer of Polaris missiles for British-built nuclear submarines. To a great many people in Britain, the British nuclear force is a wasting asset. The pace of technological change has been much faster than a country of Britain's limited though large resources can keep up with. With Polaris, there will be in any case a gap of two or three years in the late 1960's when Britain will have no strategic force. The British nuclear force has proved to have little relevance to Britain's non-European preoccupations in the Far East or Africa. Now that Britain has set her face toward Europe, she must balance the advantages of her special relationship with the United States on nuclear questions against the suspicion that this relationship engenders among her future colleagues on the Continent.

British thinking is beginning to turn more and more toward a NATO or a European focus for her nuclear effort. Consequently, there has been considerable support, except in the right wing of the Conservative Party, for those provisions of the Nassau agreement that force Britain to assign more and more of her strategic forces to NATO. It is sincerely felt that there is a strong case for an Allied nuclear striking force that is based on the European side of the Atlantic, although with better facilities for dispersal than exist in England. The reasons for this—primarily, though by no means exclusively, political and psychological—are examined in some detail below. First, it is not impossible to imagine circumstances in which such a force might be effective in validating the whole Allied deterrent, in that its mere existence and the damage —not decisive but nevertheless formidable—that it might inflict would have the effect that the Kremlin would not be prepared to gamble, as Hitler did, on a technique of piecemeal destruction. This is something quite different from the popular and highly questionable conception of "triggering off SAC" against the will of the United States. It means that in making its calculation of total war, the Kremlin would have to decide from the beginning on all (including the United States) or nothing; and it is not unreasonable to believe that it would opt for nothing.

Secondly, it is an understandable human reaction that nations

for whom the use of nuclear weapons might have utterly catastrophic results should wish to exercise some control over the policy
of that use, and have a call as of right on its protective deterrent effect. At present, no NATO partner of the United States other than
Britain has either.

Should Britain in her new position as a primarily European power
not take the lead in developing a deterrent system which is under
neither exclusive American nor exclusive British control? This is
the kind of question being asked by thoughtful people in Britain
today, as she stands on the threshold of a European relationship
and prepares to abandon her old position as a world power in special relation to the United States.

IV. The French Nuclear Force

Britain's decision to embark on an independent nuclear deterrent
had a profound effect upon France's decision to do likewise. In the
political debates that began about 1956 on the wisdom of a French
deterrent, many of the arguments put forward in British White
Papers and Parliamentary debates were imported wholesale: the
demands of national pride, the dwindling value of the American
deterrent, the necessity to possess a nuclear-weapons program to
restore France's influence within NATO. The emphasis was somewhat different in Paris from what it was in London, for, if the
British bomb was primarily intended to increase British influence
in Washington, the French bomb was aimed at destroying the very
Anglo-Saxon intimacy that the former had successfully restored. If,
during the 1950's, the British Government suffered from a certain
nostalgia for the intimacy of the Anglo-American Combined Chiefs
of Staff of wartime days, the French leaders suffered from an
equally understandable nostalgia for the early days of NATO, when
France, in the eyes of many French officials, was treated as a genuine equal of the other two powers. The increasing preoccupation
of American policy with Germany politically and with Britain militarily accentuated this feeling.

The French nuclear-weapons program ran into very heavy weather, economically and technically, and it is not improbable that the leaders of the Fourth Republic would have settled for the gift of an American nuclear submarine—making the development of this form of strength their main contribution to NATO—had it not been for the coincidence of General de Gaulle's return to power in May, 1958, and the almost simultaneous amendment of the MacMahon Act in favor of Britain but not of France. From then on, the chances of dissuading France from proceeding with her nuclear weapons were virtually nonexistent.

Yet, there still remain considerable doubts as to what purpose the French nuclear-weapons program will fulfill. A strong school of French thought contends that in default of a much more cohesive and centralized Alliance, the only deterrents that will have credibility are those under full national control. There is no doubt that President de Gaulle believes this. This same dominant school of thought argues that France needs only a small nuclear force to "tear an arm off Russia" (in De Gaulle's words) should she contemplate an attack on Europe.

But there is evidence that a great many thoughtful Frenchmen do not subscribe to this line of argument. An effective deterrent means first of all a highly sophisticated means of delivery: The aircraft that France has under development, a supersonic light bomber —the Mirage IV, which will come into service at the end of 1963— will have a very high level of performance, which would make it a useful adjunct within an over-all NATO plan. But by the mid-1960's, a means of delivery based on one type of aircraft which can barely reach targets in the Soviet Union is not going to have the necessary credibility to strengthen the position of one country by itself (though France is eventually to produce an IRBM). In recent years, the French bomb has been conceived as a form of pressure on Washington and NATO, a means of committing them to a course of action against their will. It has given France a very high nuisance value within the Alliance, though it has not increased the respect in which she is held by her allies, either across the Atlantic or in

Europe. But, equally, the United States cannot afford a prolonged period of bad relations with France, if only because of the central geographic position she occupies in Europe. Some means of meeting France's ambition to have the influence of a nuclear power must be found, within either a European or a NATO framework.

V. A European Deterrent

The problem of the European powers' control or possession of nuclear weapons cannot, however, be disposed of by casting doubts on the wisdom of current British or French policy. The expansion of the European economies and the social and political regeneration of Western Europe have coincided with evidence of the expansion of the Soviet threats, doubts about the continuing credibility of the American nuclear deterrent, and stark evidence of the unwillingness in NATO as a whole to provide the limited war forces that would make the Alliance less dependent on strategic nuclear weapons. For a while after the heads-of-government meeting in December, 1957, these anxieties were allayed by the American promises to accelerate the distribution of tactical atomic weapons, to stockpile their warheads in Europe, and to base IRBM's on European soil. But it has become increasingly apparent to European governments that the possession of tactical atomic weapons—that is, short-range ground-to-ground missiles, fighter-bombers, or artillery with nuclear warheads—gives them no control over American planning or decisions, and that the agreed system of dual control over warheads between the United States and the host country gives them no power to use tactical weapons against her will. Moreover, the vulnerable first generation of IRBM's, on whose location agreement has been reached with some countries, will have a relatively short life in the American strategy of deterrence—especially if the withdrawal of Soviet MRBM's in Cuba makes necessary reciprocal concessions on overseas bases.* There is a fear in Europe—how genuine

* The 60 Thor IRBM's located in England are to be scrapped by October, 1963. This leaves 30 Jupiter IRBM's in Italy and 15 in Turkey, which are also to be replaced. In addition, there is the 400–600-mile Pershing missile in Germany.

it is hard to tell—that the dangers of nuclear blackmail are increasing.

Conceivably, this might lead European countries other than France and Britain to consider becoming nuclear powers. But this is not the real issue. Italy, for instance, which will shortly build up large quantities of plutonium as a by-product of her big civil nuclear-energy program, is firmly committed to an Atlantic strategy, and is the foremost critic of the French approach. Similarly, Germany would face formidable obstacles if she tried to become an independent nuclear power. She would have to denounce a treaty with six Allies, as well as a solemn undertaking with the United States. She has only a research-reactor program, so that the creation of a nuclear-weapons industry would require at least five years of intensive work with minimum Allied support and maximum Soviet hostility. She has no area suitable for testing, and she has a densely crowded land area on which to base strategic weapons.*

But fear is not the only spur. As the European Community gathers strength and political cohesion, and particularly when the major European nuclear power, the United Kingdom, becomes part of it, many Europeans may conceive it to be natural that the Community, this new great power, should have its own nuclear deterrent. This view does not derive solely from European ambition: It has been fostered by the way in which successive American administrations have held out the promise that a united Europe would have the weight of a great power. And one of the central attributes of a great power is the ability to pursue an independent strategy.

Many sincere federalists in Europe, therefore, now argue for a European Community deterrent. But the clearest case for such a course was put four years ago by an American, Ben Moore, in *NATO and the Future of Europe*, a study sponsored by the Council on Foreign Relations.† In his book, Mr. Moore accepts the thesis

---

* For a fuller discussion, see Leonard Beaton and John Maddox, *The Spread of Nuclear Weapons* (London: Chatto & Windus; New York: Frederick A. Praeger; published for The Institute for Strategic Studies, 1962).

† New York: Harper & Brothers, 1958.

(which I reject) that there is a decreasing likelihood of American retaliation against a Soviet attack limited to Europe, and argues therefore for the creation of a pooled European deterrent, based on the countries of the European Economic Community and independent of the United States. He suggests that there is an identity of interest in Western Europe which can no longer be assumed to exist between Europe and America, and claims that unless there is a deterrent under strictly European control "the Europeans will continue to fear an American veto over their ability to deter a strategic attack limited to Europe, or at least fear that American hesitation will render the deterrent ineffective." Under the new system that he proposes, "NATO cohesion would not rest primarily on the certainty of the commitments between Europe and the United States, but rather on an unwritten coincidence of interests between two strong partners aligned on the same side of a new world balance of power."

There is much to attract Europeans, and those Americans who have long advocated European unity in the hope that it would relieve the United States of the burden of European defense, in this argument. It would go a considerable distance to reinforce President de Gaulle's contention that Western Europe—that is, the European Economic Community—is now a "third force" to be reckoned with in world politics. Moreover, there is much to be said for a policy of convincing Russia that Europe could act even if the United States were tied up elsewhere—say, in the Pacific. And the idea is consistent with President Kennedy's conception of an Atlantic partnership between two units of roughly equal size and weight, the United States and the European Community.

But there are a number of serious objections or obstacles to realizing any such conception within the next ten years, if by a European deterrent we mean one or more weapons systems built by the countries of the Community, financed by them, based on their soil or the adjacent seas, and under their sole control. The first objection concerns European resources for such a project. It is true that with Britain in the Community there would be no problem about nuclear warheads, since the British nuclear-weapons program is at present operating well below capacity. It is also true that the Community comprises a group of rich and resourceful countries. But it should be noted that the combined defense budgets of the Community countries (including Britain) total some $14 billion, or about one-quarter of the defense budget of the United States. To undertake the design and production of weapons systems, aircraft or missiles, that will stand up to the very rigorous conditions of the late 1960's and early 1970's would mean increasing their defense budgets by 25 per cent or else a cutback in their conventional forces. This would be the case even if European industry received some technical assistance from American industry, for few European firms have experience of this kind of research and development. Moreover, now that Algeria is independent, the only proving and testing grounds available would be in Australia or the South Pacific, which would greatly increase the cost of the finished product. And at that, it would only duplicate American deterrent resources.

In the second place, Europe is an area of very high population density, ten times higher on the average than that of the United States or western Russia. There are only two land areas in Europe suitable for basing missiles without running the risk of enormous civil casualties if they were ever attacked: a small part of the French Alps and the Scottish highlands. As the weight of Soviet warheads increases, this factor will become increasingly important. If it were decided to place a European force at sea, this would involve the same sort of problems as it would for a NATO deterrent, which we shall examine in the next section.

Third, a European system would take about six to eight years to design and bring into operation. All the plans and preparation would be more or less public knowledge from the start. During this period, the United States would presumably be less and less interested in the deterrence of attacks on Europe, while the Soviet Union would become increasingly suspicious of the growing military power of a European Community whose economic and political influences in Eastern Europe she already had good reason to fear. Would she stand idly by during this time, or might she be tempted to smash Western Europe by a timely and overwhelming blow?

The United States has now hinted that if Europe would build a truly multilateral nuclear force she would not oppose the idea.* But even if she were to help to overcome these problems—for instance, by the outright sale of advanced weapons systems—there would still be the problem of control within the European Community. According to present plans, the political community will be launched with minimal concessions of sovereignty, and may take a number of years before it even achieves a confederate structure. Yet a single system of deterrence exercised on behalf of all seven countries is politically inconceivable without a full political union: common citizenship, a common parliament, a central government, a unified army, navy, and air force, and so on. And that is many years—a decade at least—away.

Finally, it is important to remember two things. First, the European Community will not comprise all the European countries who are members of NATO. Who would continue to guarantee the integrity of Greece and Turkey, for instance? Second, the realization of a European deterrent would also be the realization of one long-standing Soviet ambition, the splitting of NATO into two halves and the division of European from American strategy.

VI. A NATO DETERRENT

In view of the shortcomings of small national deterrents and doubts about a European program, there has been considerable discussion during the past three years about the feasibility of a NATO deterrent.† The idea differs from a European deterrent in that it assumes placing part of the American deterrent system under the control of NATO itself. (The United States has never offered to

* See ·the speech by Mr. McGeorge Bundy, Special Assistant to the President on National Security Affairs, in Copenhagen on September 27, 1962.
† The first extended examination of this problem appeared in the original edition of this book (1960).

place all its deterrent systems under a NATO system; nor, since they serve a world-wide purpose, is it politically realistic to assume that she ever would.) The central purpose is that there should be part of the American system whose use does not depend on unilateral American decisions.

The proposal has been put forth in two forms. The first is General Norstad's proposal for placing an MRBM force in Europe to replace the NATO fighter bombers and medium-range aircraft as they wear out, or as their airfields become too vulnerable to Soviet interdiction. These would be mobile missiles with a 1,200–1,500-mile range under the operational command of the Supreme Commander Europe (who is, and presumably will remain, an American), but manned by international crews and operating on "guidelines" laid down by the NATO Council. The other is a proposal which has been much discussed between Washington and certain European governments to create an internationally manned fleet of surface or submarine missile ships, under the command either of the Supreme Commander Atlantic (also an American) or of a new NATO command, and operating similarly on "guidelines" laid down by the NATO Council. The former alternative could be called a tactical interdiction force, since its targets would be military objectives in Eastern Europe and its purpose to cripple an attack on Europe; the latter would be a true strategic force, probably with a counter-city deterrent role.

Of the major European NATO governments, only Germany has been seriously interested in these proposals. France has regarded them as a diversion from her objective of restoring her own position among the leading powers of the Alliance. Britain has tended to question the military and political reassurance that their implementation would bring to Europe. Opinion in the smaller countries tends to be confused or indifferent.

As far as the European MRBM force is concerned, the proposal clearly stands or falls on its military merits. It is fair to say that there is considerable skepticism as to whether SACEUR needs a force of this range at his disposal, and whether he could conceivably employ it without invoking general themonuclear war throughout the Northern Hemisphere. The German feeling is, for reasons that we shall examine in the next chapter, that the Russians should know that SACEUR, as an international military officer stationed in Europe, has just this power. Other governments feel that the decision must remain strictly a political one, and most of them are prepared to see it remain in the hands of the U.S. President.

The idea of a strategic NATO deterrent in the form of a multinational Polaris or other sea-borne missile force has been objected to on other grounds as well. In the first place, in view of the current American emphasis on controlled retaliation, the timing and nature of its use would presumably have to be entirely subordinated to American control, even if the officers who man it were not American. It is rather doubtful if an Italian or a Belgian, say, would be psychologically reassured by the American commitment to the defense of Europe merely from knowing that, somewhere out in the Atlantic or the North Sea, there is a submarine or surface ship with an Italian or Belgian officer on board. It is control that is crucial, not the manning of the weapons system, unless one makes the very dangerous assumption that the crews might take matters into their own hands.

Finally, both proposals create the same dilemma. Either the authority to use the force is delegated to a military officer, in which case governments lose their power of control in a crisis; or the power is vested in the NATO Council or some smaller body, which involves the very difficult proposition of achieving a unanimous view on the part of a number of different governments at short notice. Fifteen fingers on the safety catch—or one on the trigger. Neither formula seems the recipe for stability, or for Soviet confidence in the responsibilities, as well as the determination, of the NATO Alliance.

VII. CONTROL AND CONTRÔLE

At the present time, there is, in all the countries of the Alliance, less discussion than in recent years about the credibility of the

American strategic deterrent in the event of war in Europe. The proposition—so keenly debated by American as well as European experts—that, with the advent of full nuclear parity, the ability of the United States to take strategic action in face of a threat to her European allies is declining, has for the moment lost some of its force, and for three reasons. The first is a better appreciation of the realities of the situation, a recognition that, in the present technological context, it would be virtually impossible for the President of the United States to distinguish between a large-scale attack on Europe and the first wave of an attack likely to engulf his own country. The second is the fact that the United States is now well on the way to developing a more effective and secure retaliatory capability than seemed the case even two years ago. The third is President Kennedy's clear statements that the United States Government intends to honor its commitments, and is not making any move toward that "nuclear isolationism" which some pessimists had deduced from earlier political and technological trends.

Nevertheless, American strategic nuclear weapons remain a potential source of tension and division between the European Allies and the United States. This is not surprising: Not only are strategic nuclear weapons terrifying things to contemplate, but no system of collective security has been constructed hitherto in which the vast preponderance of strategic power remained under the unilateral control of one ally, while all were equally exposed to the strategic attack of the adversary. It is easy to make a mistake about the state of European opinion in this context, and to point to the basic ambivalence of the general European attitude—on the one hand, fear that the United States will not come to the aid of Europe, and on the other, alarm that she may take precipitate action in an emergency (the desire for a finger on the safety catch as well as on the trigger) as a reason for ignoring it.

The contradiction probably arises from superimposing one era of American strategic policy on another: Alarm at the danger of precipitate American action stems from the earlier years of the Eisenhower regime, when the doctrine of "massive retaliation" was official American policy; fear that the United States might not be able to come to Europe's aid grew up during the later Eisenhower years—especially the period of the missile muddle, when it appeared that the strategic balance of power was tilting seriously against the United States. Both fears are largely out of date, but the fact that they exist shows the weakness of the central institution. To eradicate this ambiguous thinking among America's allies requires action on two planes. First, a firm American strategic policy to meet the needs of the present day must be agreed upon; this the new administration, aided by the technical achievements of its predecessor, has now moved toward, even if there are still some inconsistencies in it to be eradicated. The second is to devise means whereby the European Allies can acquire some greater control over their own destiny in return for a greater contribution to the general strength of the Alliance.

The other source of tension is the existence of the British "independent contribution to the deterrent" in national hands, and of France's potential *force de frappe*. The two cannot be equated, for the British V-bomber force exists in considerable numbers, while the French force is still several years from completion; the operational life of the one will be continued by means of American assistance that is not likely to be forthcoming for the other. But, as purely national forces, their effects are the same. One is to encourage the diversion of defense resources from efforts in other directions—in ground, antisubmarine, and tactical air forces—that the United States, the smaller allies, and even many members of the British and French governments themselves know to have higher real priority for the security of the Alliance as a whole. The other effect is to encourage the myth that the road to influence in Washington and to prestige in the Alliance lies through the possession of nuclear weapons, and thus to make France an obdurate partner until her nuclear ambitions are satisfied.

Before considering how these two sources of malaise—ambivalence about American intentions and the resentments caused by British and French policies—can be alleviated, it is important to explain why I no longer consider that the proposal I made in the first edition of this book, written in 1959, would at present fit the needs of the case. The proposal then for creating a European-based striking force controlled by NATO itself—a NATO deterrent—was an attempt, made at a time when no constructive alternative was being considered by governments: (a) to overcome the fears that were generated in Europe, during the worst period of the missile muddle and the tail-end of the Eisenhower years, about the readiness and ability of the United States to continue to deter nuclear attack in Europe; (b) to obviate the need for a French nuclear program; (c) to mitigate the politically divisive effects of British policy when Britain was fast running down its forces in Germany while preparing to spend £600 million on the Bluestreak missile; and (d) to devise a strong central command and control system at a time when it seemed essential to construct a system of hard-based MRBM's in Europe to offset the apparent Soviet lead in ICBM's.

The idea would have been difficult to translate into practice, and considerable pragmatism and good will would have been needed to operate such a system. But the value of the idea itself has waned over the past year or so. Apart from the greater firmness of American policy, evidenced by the Kennedy Administration and based on technological developments inherited from its predecessor, it became less and less practicable as it became clear that only submarine-based missiles provided by the United States would possess sufficient invulnerability over the years to pose a strategic threat to the Soviet Union from any point outside North America. This enormously complicated the problems of command and control, eliminated any question of a new program planned and undertaken by the Alliance as a whole, and cast doubt on the value of having multilateral teams controlling the missiles.

The proposal may need reconsideration at some point in the future—for instance, if all efforts at arms control and disarmament should fail, China should become a serious nuclear power, and the United States should be forced to direct a large part of its resources to the Pacific, and thereby to ask its European allies to shoulder part of the system of strategic deterrence as well as local defense. If so, a much more drastic reconstruction of NATO might well be required to transform it from an alliance into a confederative system with institutions of supranational power.

But the debates that the idea of a NATO deterrent have generated have at least had the useful effect of illuminating a profound confusion that had existed throughout the Alliance concerning the meaning of the key word "control." NATO is a bilingual alliance, and it therefore is not surprising that the French word *contrôle*—which means examination, criticism, verification—should have become confused with the English word *control*, which in this context means physical grasp of levers and buttons. In terms of NATO, *contrôle* can be roughly equated with access to planning and policy decisions, *control* with influence over operational decisions.

If one examines the reasons that led Britain and then France to become nuclear powers, it seems to me clear that it was the desire for *contrôle* rather than *control* that was the dominant motive. Similarly, during all the anxieties of the past few years, the main desire in the other European countries, including Germany, has not been to acquire nuclear warheads or means of delivery for their own sake, so much as it has been to gain that access to and influence over the formulation of American strategic policy, especially as it affects NATO, which the possession of actual hardware gave to the British Government. The more that European governments are assured, from intimate contact with the American policy-making process, that they know what the President of the United States would do in a given situation of war or crisis, the greater will be their sense of confidence in American policy, and the freer will be his hand. The idea of fifteen heads of governments or even of their representatives consulting on the grimmest of operational decisions in the very limited time which modern high-speed delivery permits is inconceivable. But to know what the most powerful ally intends to do in an emergency, to be clear what the choices open to him are, is essential to the political cohesion of the Alliance.

It is here that a strengthened Council and a powerful civil-military Secretariat, the kind of reformed central machinery for NATO which we shall examine in Chapter 7, would make such a valuable contribution. In the creation of a strong international planning staff, a long step forward would be taken to ensure that the Council and their governments were kept fully abreast of the developments and modifications of American policy and weapons month by month. For this reason, the decision which was taken at the Athens meeting of the NATO Council in April, 1962—namely, to create a special "nuclear committee" of the Council, to which Britain and the United States will now submit their nuclear plans—is one of the most important in the history of the Alliance. How great the influence of non-American views on American strategic planning will be it is impossible to forecast, but the system will justify itself merely if European governments are fully clear as to what American policy is and is likely to be. If the NATO Council can develop into a powerful center of policy coordination and planning, and is treated with full confidence by the United States, there will be less need to contemplate giving NATO operational control over strategic weapons to create a NATO striking force.

There are two American objections to carrying this proposal very far. The first is that to accord the Alliance as a whole the kind of association with American strategic planning that Britain has enjoyed in varying degrees since NATO started might mean amending the MacMahon Act, and would certainly involve a drastic revision of official American practice and attitudes. But I find it difficult to believe that if the President made it clear to Congress that such a step would increase rather than diminish his freedom of action in an emergency, and also would ensure that American nuclear weapons remained in American hands, the Congress would fail to grasp his meaning. As to the question of security, it must be candidly pointed out that American security is almost the worst in the Alliance. To make the necessary information on American strategic planning available to the Allies is to ensure that their responsible representatives at all levels are given information in its proper perspective and setting, rather than acquiring it piecemeal from leaks in the American technical and daily press, or from the distorted statements of American senior officers intent on making a good case for more funds before Congressional committees or lobbying against the decisions of their civil superiors.

The other objection is harder to meet. It can be argued that the American policy-making process is such an untidy one, that policy evolves out of such a violent and prolonged tug of war between opposing views, services, and interests—between Congress and the White House, between the State Department and the Defense Department—that no one can say with certainty what position has been reached on any given subject at a particular time. To involve the Allies too closely in this process might mislead them and create discord rather than harmony within the Alliance. This is a real problem, but it can be overstressed.* It is true that the American policy-making process is very different from that of any European government. But as far as strategic policy is concerned, the lead time involved in modern weapons necessarily makes American planning a long-term affair. As far as more general policy is concerned, it is precisely to avoid the kind of charge of vacillation leveled from certain European quarters at the White House over the Berlin question that it is necessary to develop within NATO a policy-coordinating center where differences can be thrashed out in private at an early stage, before they become arguments between governments at the highest level and with the fullest publicity.

It is vital to maintain—as far as strategic weapons are concerned —this distinction between Allied consultation on planning and national control of operational decisions. The latter must be assumed by the national governments that possess the weapons. To deny the President the power of unfettered action in an emergency would be to rob the Western deterrent of much of its credibility. But just be-

---

* There is a case to be made for moving NATO itself to Washington so that the NATO Council could play an active part in this policy-making debate: Washington is, after all, the geographical center of the Alliance, as well as the capital of its most powerful member. However, in view of the fact that a distinctive European consciousness is emerging and that the United States may have to ask Europe to share some of its burdens, Paris still seems the best center.

cause this is so, his allies must know in advance which alternative courses are open to him. Moreover, if the United States is prepared to treat NATO as an essential part of the planning and consultative mechanism for the evolution of her own strategic planning, she can avoid the dilemma of either having to hand over control of some of her strategic weapons to her Allies, or else having a number of nervous Allied prime ministers on the telephone or on the steps of the White House in time of crisis.

Such an initiative would, equally, provide a means of reconciling the British, and later the French, nuclear capability with the requirements of the Alliance. Clearly, the statesmanlike course would be for the United States to put that part of its strategic nuclear forces still based in Europe, including the Seventh Fleet, under the planning control of a reorganized NATO, on condition that the United Kingdom did likewise with her Bomber Command. Both countries could be protected by a provision that—in the event of conflict in one of their other treaty areas, SEATO or CENTO— they could withdraw their European-based nuclear forces (all British nuclear forces are normally European-based) by agreement with the NATO Council. These forces would remain under national command in peacetime, but their deployment and potential employment would cease to be a closed secret between Washington and London, between British Bomber Command and SAC, and form part of the whole NATO plan, subject to the *contrôle* of the Council through the new "nuclear committee."* If it became clear, as I think it would, that the real channel of British military influence in Washington lay through the NATO machinery and the appointments held by her representatives in its Secretariat, the incentive to prolong the life of a British strategic deterrent in order to preserve her special American connection would diminish. As economic and technological factors force her to move from strategic to tactical nuclear delivery systems, intended for European rather than world-wide purposes, Britain could continue to play a special-

---

* This arrangement seems very similar to the general provisions of the Nassau agreement between President Kennedy and Prime Minister Macmillan of December, 1962, which was reached just before this book went to press.

ized nuclear role in the defense of Europe without having to claim a special status within the Alliance.

It can be argued that no British or American decision at this stage will affect French policy. I am not sure that this is true. What is true, at this moment, is that no such initiative would affect President de Gaulle's views on the development of the *force de frappe*. If, however, his allies can, in the year or so before it becomes truly operational, demonstrate that a framework of Allied planning has been created into which such a force can be accepted without any loss of French influence or prestige, then the monetary costs of the *force de frappe*—inevitably higher than the original forecasts—plus the clear demonstration of its insignificant diplomatic value as a purely national force could well create a change in French policy. The Mirage IV, France's contender for nuclear great-power status, could then be given the same kind of specialized tactical role in European defense as the British TSR2. It is asking a great deal of Britain and France to accept the fact that even as nuclear powers they cannot maintain the status of strategic powers. It involves the abandonment of any idea that they can pursue a worldwide strategy, or even maintain the status of nominal equality with the United States that they were accorded when NATO was founded. But they will be faced with a choice not only between being strategic or merely local nuclear powers, but also between accepting a reality—and thereby reducing friction and suspicion within the Alliance to a minimum—or maintaining a fiction that could do continuing damage to its political and psychological cohesion.

But it is clear that any such formula depends absolutely on whether the United States uses the new "nuclear committee" of the Council as part of her own planning machinery, and consults, not merely informs, her allies at every stage of the formulation of strategic planning. It is only by this means that the differential between nuclear and nonnuclear powers within the Alliance can be prevented from generating envy, dread, and most of the other deadly sins that lead to the decay of alliances.

6

INTERDEPENDENCE AND EUROPEAN
SECURITY

I

Europe, as has been said earlier, is the primary preoccupation of
the Alliance. And there are many students of the European scene
who believe that the present policy of the Alliance with regard to
Europe is too conservative, too inflexible, too concerned with an improbable Soviet attack instead of the more constructive task of developing, on a basis of common interest, a generally acceptable
political solution to the deadlock in Europe. The proposals for
eliciting this common interest vary, but in general they have centered around a scheme of either "disengagement," "denuclearization," or "thinning out" in the middle of Europe, in the interests of
a united Germany and of a Soviet withdrawal from Eastern Europe.
If these were negotiable propositions in the immediate future,
much of the current preoccupation in NATO about the strength
of the "shield" force and its related problems would be irrelevant.
One purpose of this study is to suggest that until a greater degree of
unity is made evident in NATO, and energetic steps are taken to
redress the tactical balance within Europe, the materials for a successful negotiation with the Soviet Union may be too scanty to
give good prospects of success.

The problem of negotiation has two aspects—political and mili-

tary. The tensions that a confrontation with the hard facts of interdependence are causing at the present time in NATO are so severe
that—contrary to the current fears of some European countries—no
Soviet leader would enter into any agreement on Europe with the
United States alone, lest the mere act of doing so would cause it
to be upset by some European leaders, who now play the same
negative role in NATO as China does in the Soviet system of alliances. As long as there is no attempt to reach fundamental agreement on the interests of the West, which means deciding what
can be relinquished as well as what cannot, something that requires
continuous international consultation rather than occasional meetings of foreign ministers—NATO can be nothing but inflexible.

The other precondition of success is a better military balance in
Europe and a Western strategy more flexible than primary reliance
on nuclear weapons. It is a fact that Western interest in arms-
control measures for Europe increased as the strategic balance of
power became more open to question. The converse is also true:
the Soviet Union was most interested in such ideas in the years
1952–55, when the Western military position was at its strongest.
At this moment, Soviet interest in a European settlement is probably at its lowest. The point is to revive it—and by less dangerous
means than frightening the Soviet Union with the specter of a
nuclear-armed West Germany.

Few people in NATO today—whatever eventual settlement they
have in their mind's eye—would deny the importance of a strong
and flexible conventional force in Western Europe. The striking
thing is the gap between acceptance and performance. In the five
or six years since the NATO governments first began to realize the
need for a greater limited-war capability in Europe, the United
Kingdom has reduced her contribution to those forces by the equivalent of a division, or a quarter of her effective fighting strength;
France, even now that the end of the Algerian crisis has enabled her
to reorganize her forces, has made no attempt to restore her contribution to anything like its original level of four divisions; and the

quantitative contribution of most of the smaller countries is static. Since the concept of interdependence is still so shallowly rooted in public psychology, one can hardly blame the smaller NATO countries for setting their course to conform to the line taken in London and Paris. The consequence is that any hope of raising the level of the ground forces to even twenty-six divisions, out of the thirty that SHAPE stated was a minimum requirement, rests entirely on the efforts of Germany—and even then, it can only be done if the United States maintains her present contribution of five divisions.

The reasons for this contradiction between words and behavior are clear enough. European public opinion is very unwilling to face the fact that the validity of the nuclear deterrent, whether it be purely American or developed along the interdependent lines suggested in the last chapter, is now linked to a capacity for local defense. Europeans have lived for so long under the umbrella of American strategic air power that it takes a major effort of will to adjust their thinking to an era in which it is no longer a sufficient answer. Conventional forces are expensive to maintain—they are not only politically but socially unpopular in Europe—and since an average of two-thirds of government expenditure in Europe is committed to other services besides defense, such as education and welfare (as against three-eights in the United States), a major rise in conventional defense expenditure would mean a proportionate increase in taxes.

Moreover, the particular difficulty of inspiring support for the "shield" is that it is essentially a contingency force. The role of a bomber or missile crew with a nuclear bomb or warhead can be defined precisely—in fact, must be, for it has only one function to perform. But no one can say exactly what function the components of the "shield" force will be called upon to perform—to play a vital but sanguinary role in the first forty-eight hours of a major nuclear war, to police a border scuffle, or never to fight at all. It is an index of the flexibility of conventional forces—army, navy, or air—that their exact role can never be defined in advance.

II

We have seen earlier that the fears of the late 1950's that the United States might be entering a period of decisive strategic inferiority to the Soviet Union have proved to be groundless. Measured in terms of destructive potential, the two nations have an equally powerful stranglehold on each other.

But the new situation is creating a different relationship between the United States and her allies, and already imposes a different set of military requirements on the Alliance as a whole from those that obtained during the supremacy of the medium bomber and before the Soviet nuclear stockpile attained its present size. It does not mean that the integrity or the effectiveness of the American commitment to the defense of Europe in the event of major attack is weakening.* It must not be forgotten that the American signature to the North Atlantic Treaty was not an act of disinterested generosity, but derived from a well-thought-out decision that the survival of Western Europe was essential to the survival of the United States itself. Nothing has happened to alter that judgment, and now that the protagonists of "agonizing reappraisal" have had their day and a clearer vision of the American national interest has been restored in Washington, it is apparent that any talk of American withdrawal from Europe to a "fortress America" position was always a hollow bluff. If there were any doubt about it, President Kennedy's decision not only to maintain the present level of American forces in Europe, despite the drain on the foreign-exchange resources of the United States, but also to reinforce them in a crisis should finally dispose of any such questions in Washington, Europe, and Moscow.

Nevertheless, the advent of nuclear parity has profoundly altered the nature of the American guarantee to Europe. The existence even of an effective, well-protected, strategic retaliatory force can

---

* For an authoritative examination of this fact, see Albert Wohlstetter, "Nuclear Sharing: NATO and the N+1 Country Problem," *Foreign Affairs*, April, 1961.

no longer deter all forms of threat to Europe. As the counter-force capability of the United States diminishes in relation to the growth and diversification of Soviet long-range striking power, so the deterrent value of the threat of massive nuclear retaliation against anything short of a massive attack on Europe and the United States must diminish with it; in other words, strategic nuclear weapons must increasingly become a deterrent only to the use of their Soviet counterparts. Now that both sides have a continuous spectrum of weapons of mass destruction in their armories, the kind of limited challenge presented by a crisis over Berlin or on the line of the Iron Curtain, by a threat to northern Norway, the Baltic Straits, or Greece (let alone in Southeast Asia or the Middle East) can be met only at the level at which it is offered. To rest the defense of Europe on a force that could withstand a military challenge only for a few hours without resorting to nuclear weapons is likely to lead to insecurity and diplomatic paralysis.

One reason it has taken so long for governments and military leaders to accept the logic of events has been the attempt to build around the tactical atomic weapon a doctrine of limited atomic war. NATO governments were all the more ready to engage in such an exercise, partly because of the historic dislike in some countries of large standing armies, partly because of the widely held belief that the disbursement of tactical atomic weapons to the European Allies gave them a measure of control over American policy. Moreover, army staffs have seen in this development an opportunity, hitherto reserved for air forces and navies, to graft their tactics on to the most advanced and spectacular developments in military science. The consequence has been that the NATO ground forces in the Central Area have increasingly been trained and organized for atomic warfare only, a military posture that is at worst highly dangerous in terms of miscalculation, and at best probably irrelevant to the kinds of challenge to Western nerve, morale, and clear judgment that are likely to arise.

At the same time, the belief that it would be possible to fight a war in Europe in which nuclear weapons were confined to battle-

field targets, without incurring an impossibly high risk of escalation into thermonuclear strategic war, is dying a slow but sure
death, for two reasons which Henry A. Kissinger, originally one of
the chief architects of the theory of limited nuclear war, has candidly and courageously pointed out in his recent book, *The Necessity for Choice.** It has proved impossible, he argues, to develop an
agreed interservice doctrine on what limitations could be accepted
and observed once nuclear weapons had been introduced into the
battle. And the development of the medium-range missile and the
nuclear-armed fighter-bomber increases the potential depth of the
battlefield to a point where both adversaries would find it very
difficult to determine whether—in, say, Poland or the Low Countries—they were being subjected to interdiction attack or to the first
wave of strategic bombing aimed at their heartlands.

The Kennedy Administration deserves great credit for grappling
with this problem of the overdependence of NATO's European
defenses on nuclear weapons so soon after taking office. The President's action in making clear that there would be no reduction in
American ground forces in Europe—and that there might even be
an increase in times of emergency—should remove any fear that
the American desire to see stronger indigenous conventional forces
there is the first step in some policy of withdrawal. But it is essential to keep the problem of strengthening the NATO "shield" in
proper perspective. In the first place, no one has suggested, and
there seems no valid military requirement for, a dramatic increase
in the size of the NATO "shield" force in the Central Area. If
one accepts current NATO doctrine—which seems to me sound
in this respect—that the role of the NATO ground forces is not to
fight a prolonged battle for the defense of Europe so much as it
is to hold conflict at the lowest possible level for the longest possible time (perhaps two days, perhaps a week) in order to win a
breathing space for considered political decisions by both sides on
the implications of mounting to a higher level of warfare, then
the figure of thirty divisions stationed in the Central Area in nor-

* New York: Harper & Brothers, 1961.

mal times is adequate.* By this, I mean full-strength divisions and not the shadowy skeletons that too often pass muster in the NATO order of battle. If that figure were reached, as it could be with the completion of the German program and the honoring by Britain and France of their original commitments of four divisions, it would represent a numerical superiority of three to two over the Soviet divisions normally stationed in the German Democratic Republic. It is quite true that during 1961 and 1962, Mr. Khrushchev on a number of occasions tried to convince public opinion in the NATO countries that attempts to improve their conventional strength were worthless, since he had only to snap his fingers to summon up much greater reserves. He arrested the decrease in the size of Soviet ground forces that had been announced in January, 1960 (this policy was probably suspended late in 1960 or early in 1961, and possibly for reasons unconnected with the Berlin crisis), and he lowered the Russian draft age from eighteen to seventeen. But the economic and social pressures that had originally made him anxious to reduce Soviet mobilized manpower are still as strong as ever, and it is reasonable to assume that his actions are designed to have a short-term effect and do not represent a permanent change in Soviet policy.

But by the same token, it is essential, in terms of strong Western diplomacy and morale, that it be possible to augment the NATO forces in Central Europe above their present level of about 24 divisions and 4,000 aircraft, in order to register determination by nonprovocative means during limited periods of high tension. And this requires an increase in the strategic reserves of the leading NATO powers, for it is only they who can put a significant number of efficient additional forces into Europe on rela-

---

* Neither side will accept defeat in Europe without recourse to nuclear weapons. Conventional forces there are essentially an arms-control device to prevent nuclear war from breaking out. This is the point that seems to elude President de Gaulle when he tells his visitors that French troops will only fight to the death under French command and for French soil. Similarly, many Germans tend to equate conventional war in Europe with the full horrors of World War II. A prolonged conventional war in Europe, testing the last ounce of national morale and will, is an inconceivable state of affairs.

tively short notice. Since—given the present state of British commitments elsewhere—it is really only the United States (and to a lesser extent France) that can provide a strategic reserve large enough to have real diplomatic significance, how does this affect the need to redistribute European and American shares of NATO's common burdens? The answer, to my mind, lies in terms not so much of quantity as of quality.

The quality of the non-American units in Germany is uneven in terms of equipment, training, mobility, and efficiency—discrepancies of which the Russians are keenly aware. The United States would find a readier response from the allies to a demand for improvement in the training, manning, and equipment of their conventional forces, so that they matched the high standard of the American forces (using economic resources with which they are now for the most part liberally endowed), than to a demand that they markedly increase their size, since manpower suitable and available for military service is even scarcer in Europe than in the United States. (Even so, this might require significant changes in the manpower policy of several NATO allies, since high-quality units inevitably create a demand for technicians and highly qualified men who are now scarce all over Europe.) For it is an irony of the present situation that the United States, with a high wartime birth rate, increasing automation in industry, endemic unemployment, and a selective-service system, can augment her conventional forces more easily—in a political sense—than most European countries. However, to ask the United States permanently to station still larger conventional forces in Europe would be disastrous to mutual confidence and respect within the Alliance. To ask her to maintain her present commitment and improve her reserve commitment in return for a rapid improvement of the efficiency of the European NATO forces is the more reasonable equation. It would be a double irony if the European partners were unable to meet their half of the bargain, when one considers that in the earlier part of this century the German, British, and French armies were the most efficient in the world, while the American army was an ill-paid, socially despised, and minuscule force. Moreover, some

European countries are now making important advances in conventional weapons such as antitank missiles. If the European Allies cannot match American forces in quality, then the equitable and psychologically unifying course would be to contribute a greater proportion of the cost of maintaining them in Europe.

In the second place, few responsible people have suggested that NATO can wholly dispense with shorter-range nuclear weapons or contemplate resting the security of Europe on conventional forces alone. The continued presence of such weapons in Europe is necessary: first, to deter their use by Soviet forces in any minor war situation in Europe, and second, to remove any temptation for the Soviet Union to take a leaf from the pages of German history and present the United States and Britain with the *fait accompli* of a conquered Western Europe—by means of a swift offensive in the manner of May, 1940, using her strong tactical air power to reinforce her limited strength on the ground. The essential point is that weapons such as Honest John, Sergeant, Pershing, and the nuclear-armed fighter-bombers should be regarded as a form of penultimate reserve firepower to be employed only—but only—when it is clear that massive aggression, conventional or nuclear, is under way, and not as part of the resources that divisional or subordinate commanders would expect to have available to them in the early stages of combat. Since they are purely American weapons—launcher as well as warhead—perhaps they should have been concentrated in special American units under the direct command of the commanders-in-chief of the central and southern areas (they are not deployed in the northern area), to be used only on the highest political authority.* But the policy of devolving them has gone so

---

* It is interesting to learn that the German Government originally held the same view. Herr Strauss explained recently: "We asked the Americans years ago whether—in order to avoid the problem of arming the Bundeswehr with these weapons systems, with carriers to be fitted with warheads in emergencies, and still maintain the same firepower along the entire front line—they were prepared to incorporate American artillery and rocket battalions into German divisions: Then Germans would not be equipped with atomic weapons." The American reply was that for budgetary and organizational reasons, this was impossible. See "A New Army for the New Germany," by George Bailey, *The Reporter*, July 20, 1961.

far that it would be difficult to reverse it and to correct some of the
false premises on which the training of national forces—most particularly the British and German armies—has proceeded, without
immediately carrying the opposite policy to its logical conclusion.
One should, therefore, be content for the present to see army
nuclear support weapons held under the authority of corps or
army group commanders but no lower in the chain of command.

III

The view I have just expressed represents that of most Americans, many people in Britain, and some on the Continent.* But in
recent years a very different attitude to the relation between conventional forces and nuclear weapons has grown up on the Continent and especially in Germany.

As viewed from Germany, the chief danger of the age of nuclear
parity is that it may tempt the Russians to attack some limited or
exposed part of Germany's already small land area—Lübeck in the
north, for instance, or Stuttgart in the south, Hamburg or Frank-
furt. Whereas the British and the Americans are increasingly preoccupied with the dangers of nuclear war by miscalculation or by
the rapid escalation of a minor clash into a full-scale thermonuclear
exchange, the Germans chiefly fear some nonnuclear *promenade
militaire* by the Russians that the other Western nuclear powers
would not be prepared to risk their own destruction to repulse.
Their nightmare is that the great powers would agree to halt a
war after the Russians were 50 miles inside German territory. They
therefore consider it essential that the Russians have no confidence
that they could even put one soldier across the Iron Curtain without running a very high risk of starting a nuclear war. This is not
to say that the Germans insist that nuclear weapons must be used
in such a contingency, but rather that the Russians must have no
certainty that they would not. Consequently, Herr Strauss, the

---

* See General Etienne Valluy, *Se defendre?* (Paris: Librairie Plon, 1960);
and Helmut Schmidt, *Defense or Retaliation* (London: Oliver & Boyd, 1962;
New York: Frederick A. Praeger, 1962).

former German Defense Minister, has firmly resisted the Anglo-American school of thought, and has pointed out that if the danger of escalation is a worry to the great powers, it is one of the chief protections of exposed countries like Germany. (In this argument, he has the support of many French and other European leaders.) He is anxious to retain tactical atomic weapons as an integral part of the forward divisions in Germany, and even to devise a system whereby, in an acute emergency, the forward commanders could use them without American sanction on the authority of the country under actual or potential attack.

As a head-on clash between dynamic defense ministers—Strauss on the one hand and McNamara on the other—the Anglo-Saxon and the Continental views might appear irreconcilable. This is precisely the weakness of NATO—namely, that there is no provision for continuous international planning. Statements by President Kennedy, Mr. McNamara, and other leading American officials about European defense over the past two years tend to imply that when the United States changes its policy, the rest of the Alliance should conform. But this is the language of a bygone age, before the European countries had regained strong governments and strong views of their own.

In fact, there are several ways in which a truly international planning staff could seek to reconcile these two divergent points of view—through continuous study, joint exercises, and the like. One way, for instance, would be to examine the feasibility of a militia-type defense for the forward countries, based on the new light weapons and antitank missiles. If workable, this would free the twenty-six divisions from having to hold every inch of the Iron Curtain line; it would restore mobility to their operations, and enable them to concentrate a powerful force to repel any limited grab for Lübeck or Hamburg without recourse to tactical nuclear weapons.

Another line of possible reform would be to revise the air planning for NATO so as to concentrate more conventional air and missile power in support of the defending forces instead of on interdiction targets, airfields, or missile bases deep in Eastern Europe. The interdiction role—which would be implemented only if all hope of restraining conflict below the nuclear level had to be abandoned—could be assumed by the American missiles (when they become sufficiently reliable) operating from the United States under the new controlled-reprisal doctrine.

Another approach would be to concentrate resources on vastly improved communication and command systems, so that senior commanders and national leaders could have a clear and continuous picture of the nature and scope of any conflict. They would not then have to rely on the slow piecing together of information through traditional command systems.

But to find such constructive ways of reconciling the conflicting needs and fears of different members of the Alliance, who stand in a different geographic relationship to the potential threat, the normal techniques of sporadic intergovernmental negotiation are quite inadequate.

IV

The tactics of the nuclear and the conventional battlefields are very different, and it will not be easy for commanders to readapt their training to new techniques. It is hard not to feel considerable sympathy with European politicians and military commanders— in Germany and elsewhere—who, having originally accepted the necessity of tactical atomic weapons with reluctance, are now asked to reverse the premises on which their planning and training for the last six or seven years were based. It might be easier to accept the necessity for such an alteration if greater emphasis were also laid on another major priority of Alliance planning—progress on arms control. Too much of NATO's military planning has proceeded in a political vacuum, without reference to the broader requirements of international stability. The need to find ways of checking the upward spiral of arms and forces and of eliminating the most likely causes of war is now very much in the minds of all the political leaders of the NATO powers—most particularly since the tense weeks of Soviet-American exchanges over Cuba in October, 1962. At the same time, it is evident that the requirements of stability dictate that such restraints do not depend only on the successful outcome of complex or protracted multilateral negotiations with the Soviet Union, but that they be initiated by unilateral action on both sides. It is belatedly coming to be recognized that arms control and military planning are not antithetical but are two facets of the same policy.

In the context of NATO, this has two special implications. The first is that, as the more radical approaches to the problem of arms control run into technical or political objections, it may prove necessary to make a start with some form of agreed limitation of armaments, particularly of nuclear weapons in Europe, the area that both sides rightly regard as the one where war could most easily erupt. If this is the case, NATO must work toward a military posture that makes it possible to contemplate such a proposal. (This is one of the weaknesses of General Norstad's proposals for an IRBM force in Europe.)

The second requirement of arms control is to evolve the clearest and most watertight system of command over nuclear weapons, in order to convince the adversary that we are doing everything that human ingenuity can devise to mitigate the dangers of war through accident, irresponsibility, or miscalculation. A declared policy of concentrating the physical control of tactical nuclear weapons in Europe at the highest efficient level of responsibility (as the Russians themselves claim to do) might have a valuable effect in adjusting the distorted Soviet perspective on NATO military planning. Moreover, a greater concern for the place of arms control in military planning would give a constructive, rather than a purely defensive, complexion to the central institutions of the Alliance.

7

THE EVOLUTION OF A
COMMON POLICY

I

In the early days of NATO, the principal emphasis of the Allied governments was on the speediest possible development of central military commands. The central political institutions, the NATO Council with its fifteen permanent representatives and the office of the Secretary-General and his staff, were developed more slowly, and until 1956 or 1957 were considered by the member governments to be less important. The shock of the Suez debacle gave rise to the Committee of Three, and on their recommendation the powers of the Secretary-General were enhanced and the Council's terms of reference were widened to include questions outside the NATO area. But despite these reforms, neither the Council nor the NATO Secretariat wields the authority or is equipped for the responsibilities that the need for a high degree of political coordination imposes.

What are these responsibilities? They seem to divide into two categories—those concerned with the direct confrontation of the Soviet Union in Europe, and those deriving from the need to maintain a stable pattern of international relationships in the rest of the world.

Now it would be absurd to suggest that the NATO Council does not spend a great deal of its time in considering questions of European security. The fact that it does, that the representatives of the smaller or more exposed European powers are in constant touch with American, British, or French views and support, partly accounts for the fact that Soviet attempts to apply pressure and blackmail on them in turn have met with only marginal success.

But regular consultation on problems or threats as they arise is one thing; joint planning is quite another. Two points cannot fail to impress the outside observer of the operations of NATO. The first is that the NATO Council in Paris has little authority over the military planning of either the Standing Group and the Military Committee in Washington or of their most dynamic subordinate command, Supreme Headquarters Europe. The Council is consulted, it is informed, it is advised by the military authorities as occasion serves, but it does not wield a real authority over the work of the international military institutions of the Alliance that is in any way comparable to that which national cabinets wield over national military planning. The Council thus has little power to determine the military environment in which it may be asked to reach political judgments. Because of this, it can only function, for the most part, as a clearinghouse for individual national aspirations and anxieties.

In the second place, the permanent NATO Secretariat is not a strong enough body to undertake effective long-range planning on behalf of the Alliance. Except in certain specialized and technical financial fields, governments have not encouraged the formation of a civil staff with a caliber high enough to act as an international policy-coordination center that will earn the respect of governments in the way that the staff of OEEC has done or the new "Eurocrats" in the central institutions of the European Economic Community are earning it.

It may be argued that this is a false analogy, that it is impossible to attempt long-range or detailed political planning in the same way in which it has proved both necessary and possible for international staffs to make long-range economic forecasts or military plans. This is true of many aspects of politics and diplomacy, but not all. In Europe especially, there are certain intractable or endemic problems (made intractable as much by differences among the allies as between the Alliance and Russia) that call for the kind of continuing concentration that only a high-class staff can bring to bear. It was, for instance, a rude shock to discover that virtually no international staff work was done on the Berlin problem between the ending of the 1958–59 crisis and the recrudescense of the Soviet threat to Berlin in the spring of 1961.

A crucial area of policy to which NATO, as an institution, has made virtually no contribution is arms control and those aspects of disarmament policy that would affect Europe. Yet this is as central to the aims and responsibilities of the Alliance as military planning, and in many ways is much more difficult. Because there is no central staff in the NATO Secretariat permanently at work on these problems, the plans formulated, often hastily, by national governments have more than once foundered because of hostility of other member governments to them (perhaps because their officials have not devoted consistent attention to the problem) or else because of the natural caution of international military staffs.* A great deal of consistent attention is now devoted to arms control and disarmament policy by the United States Government and in American universities. But little of this is communicated to other governments in NATO, without whose support the United States is unlikely to make much headway with the Soviet Union or in the United Nations. As far as the application of American ideas is concerned, one can be quite certain that a common policy cannot be evolved without the creation of a joint staff to work on it, and NATO is clearly the right place to create such a team.

Still another field in which the views of NATO (the civil institution, as distinct from SHAPE, the military headquarters) carry little weight is the evaluation of trends in the policies of the Soviet

---

* It must be said in justice to the NATO military staffs that they have done their very best to fill the gap left by the weakness of the NATO Secretariat and to do some serious work on arms control themselves.

Union or of other countries potentially hostile to the Alliance. By this, I do not mean either purely military intelligence or intelligence gathering, which is so delicate a task that it can probably only be conducted by national governments. What I do mean is the evaluation of intentions and broad trends of Soviet and Communist policy by competent experts. One often hears an official of one NATO government bewailing the fact that another government places quite a different interpretation on Soviet policy, and ascribing difficulties in achieving joint action or a common outlook to this cause. In so far as this can be corrected, NATO is clearly the place to make the attempt, not by occasional conferences, but with an influential international staff continually considering the evidence. Here the blurring of the old distinction between the great and the lesser powers is relevant; with their widening interests, the smaller NATO powers now often have important insights to contribute to the views of the larger powers.

II

On questions of European and Atlantic security, it seems to me that events have demonstrated clearly that intergovernmental consultation alone is no longer adequate to the demands of the 1960's, and that nothing less than the evolution of a system of joint political planning by a strong international staff will give governments the necessary foundation on which to develop a more unified policy.* But the problem of dealing with situations outside the NATO area is more complex.

The need for a unified policy in this regard is obvious, for, as the world shrinks, the extent to which the unilateral action of one NATO power directly affects the interests and security of the others increases sharply. The events of recent years provide direct evidence of this. The failure of Belgium to launch the Congo as a viable sovereign state and the chaos that ensued not only compli-

* For an interesting analogy in the field of international economic planning, see Lord Franks, "Cooperation Is Not Enough," *Foreign Affairs*, July, 1962.

cated the task and jeopardized the authority of the U.N. (on whose effective functioning all the members of NATO depend, though President de Gaulle may at present think otherwise) but also jeopardized British and French relationships with their Commonwealth and Community associates in Africa. Conversely, the pace of British and French policies in Africa has had a profound effect on the positions of Belgium and Portugal. American policy in Latin America—and not just in Cuba—now increasingly affects the interests of her NATO allies there, just as her Asian and African policies interact with theirs. And the failure of France and the United States to coordinate their policies in the successor states of Indochina during the past seven years has harmed not only those two countries, but the West as a whole, and has made of Southeast Asia a focal point of the Cold War.

There is no simple answer here. To suggest that the same kind of joint planning should be developed as for questions of European policy would be—even if it were acceptable to the NATO governments concerned—a mistake. The new countries—most particularly in Africa—are intensely suspicious of any effort to devise a monolithic Western policy toward them. An overt attempt to create "a political general staff," as some Americans and Europeans have suggested, would do considerably more harm than good. At the same time, the hopes still nourished in many NATO countries that somehow or other it can be made clear to the uncommitted world that NATO is concerned purely with the confrontation of Russia, and that membership in it does not imply support for the policies of allies in other parts of the world, are proving a delusion.

This does not mean that NATO should try to plan a collective policy for action in the non-NATO world. But it does mean that its member governments now have an absolute duty to inform their allies, and to submit, through the NATO Council, their policies and plans for action in other parts of the world to the collective judgment of allies whose interests are more and more closely interrelated. It could be argued that this can be done through the ordinary process of diplomacy. But collective judgments are sometimes more valuable than individual ones. The present Belgian Government now wisely takes the line that it would prefer to have its African policy actively criticized in the NATO Council than to have it heard in polite silence by its allies and then to see them vote against it at the U.N. The United States might have been deterred from its Cuban folly in 1961 if it had ever asked its NATO Allies to help it assess the balance of risks in the Caribbean (just as the British and French decision to make war on Egypt in 1956 would never have survived discussion in the NATO Council). In the Cuban crisis of October, 1962, the clear and present danger presented by the buildup of Soviet missiles on Cuba probably justified the United States in enforcing a blockade without consulting, but merely informing, her NATO Allies. However, the American representatives had been keeping the NATO Council secretly briefed on American fears and suspicions about Soviet action in Cuba for several months before the crisis broke. It can also be argued that to accept such a commitment to consult one's allies would lead to inaction and paralysis on the part of the major powers. I find this argument unconvincing. For one thing, there is no virtue in action for its own sake, and there is a high premium on avoiding rash action outside the NATO area. For another, in the delicate balance of contemporary international affairs, it is unlikely that the acts of the leading NATO powers in Africa, the Middle East, or Asia will achieve their purpose unless they have the support of their Atlantic allies.

At present, Angola presents in many ways as difficult a problem for the Alliance as Berlin does. There may be a justification for Dr. Salazar's colonial policy, but it is hard to discern it; its basic assumptions and the methods used to enforce them are in flat contradiction to those that govern the aims and actions of the other colonial powers in NATO and the noncolonial allies, who are almost as closely affected. Portugal may have to be persuaded to change the whole foundation of her colonial policy if the word NATO is not to stink in African nostrils and all the member countries are not to suffer in greater or lesser degree. Yet where can the resolution of these conflicting views and interests be reached if not in the NATO Council? Unlike the U.N., its deliberations are private and discreet; it comprises those countries on whose good will the security and prosperity of Portugal wholly depend; and it can, if it must, wield the ultimate sanction of expulsion, for Portugal's military contribution to NATO is negligible, and her strategic value now greatly diminished. If the Allies cannot persuade Portugal to modify her colonial policy, then world opinion—Communist, nonaligned, or even in the NATO countries themselves—can only conclude that the political institutions of the Alliance are mere façades.

I do not mean to suggest that consultation on wider problems or on those outside the NATO area should in any way be given priority over the evolution of a common policy on European questions or those concerned with the military confrontation of the Soviet Union. Any such idea would be absurd. But the one is essential to the other, in the sense that the smaller countries in the Alliance can be expected to have a degree of confidence in NATO, to give its interests a high priority in their planning, to accept the risks as well as benefits which membership confers, only if it gives them access to the American, British, and French policy-making process and an opportunity to exert an influence on it over a wide range of questions—in a way that the mere conventional diplomatic intercourse of friendly countries would not. Since their world-wide interests are increasingly extended, an intimate knowledge of the factors that may decide American policy toward, say, Southeast Asia or British policy in the Persian Gulf has a distinct bearing on their readiness to face the strains of a Berlin crisis. Moreover, there are broad questions of national policy to which a proper answer can only be given after candid discussion in NATO. One obvious one at present is whether Britain should try to help keep the peace in the Middle East and Far East by maintaining nearly half her forces there at great cost, or whether she should concentrate her strength more in Europe. The argument is a finely balanced one, in terms of the interests of the Allies as well as for Britain, but I doubt if it can be satisfactorily solved by national discussion alone.

The third reform of the political machinery of NATO concerns the status of the members of the Council. For the past ten years, the NATO countries have, for the most part, appointed professional diplomats as their permanent representatives on the Council. The value of the NATO Council is enormous, for it is the only body of Western political representatives that meets regularly every week or more often (in addition to the spring and December meetings of foreign ministers). Important subjects can thus be discussed by men who have a thorough knowledge of each others' minds, and without creating the sense of crisis that special gatherings of ministers or officials from different capitals tend to cause. But it is doubtful whether, if the Secretariat is to be strengthened, and the terms of reference of the Council widened so that it acquires certain operational responsibilities, professional diplomats can carry enough weight with their own governments and with public opinion in their nations to make the Council the influential center of discussion and decision that the course of events now demands. Skillful and experienced as professionals may be in dealing with the agenda of the Council, there seems to me a strong case for appointing men with political standing in their own country who can speak directly to the heads of governments and, where constitutionally possible, to parliaments. There is no question of abandoning the extremely useful rules of privacy that govern discussion in the Council: The point is to have a man who can convince his own nation by direct means that the interests of his country have not been overlooked in reaching a decision that may not be wholly palatable, after full and candid discussion with his peers.

The arrangement would differ according to the constitutional practice of different countries. In those with a parliamentary and cabinet government, such as Britain, Canada, Belgium, Norway, and Denmark, it would presumably involve the appointment of a minister of state or a minister for North Atlantic affairs as the permanent representative on the NATO Council, perhaps with a seat in the Cabinet. In the United States, it would mean the appointment of a special representative of the President, who either would be a member of the National Security Council *in absentia* or would report directly to it in the same way that Mr. Adlai Stevenson and his predecessors have reported directly from the United Nations (the appointment of the present American Ambassador to NATO, Mr. Thomas Finletter, who has been an influential political figure at home, meets this requirement halfway). In the France of the Fifth Republic and those countries that are governed by one man, it would involve the appointment of someone high in his confidence. This is not a reform that is likely to take place overnight: The point is that if several of the leading NATO countries appointed men of this caliber, the others would feel bound to follow suit.

Since the countries of the Alliance are not yet prepared to take a step toward creating a federation, since the NATO Council is in fact a permanent grouping of national delegates, there is no question of giving a revised Council any supranational powers. The point is to enhance its status in the eyes of governments, electorates, and adversaries so that its declarations and recommendations have the maximum impact on the course of events. The professional diplomat should remain on the national delegation, for his advice will be invaluable if the Council's terms of reference are enlarged, but the chief representative should be a figure of political weight. It is only by this means that NATO can respond swiftly to diplomatic probes and avert, for instance, the tardy and ragged response that was all the Western powers could make to the closing of the East Berlin frontier on August 13, 1961. In times of high tension, it is probably necessary to establish a political operations center akin to a military command post, if the inherent disadvantage of a large alliance facing a single adversary is to be overcome. In a democratic alliance, this can only be manned by figures who command political support in their own countries.

III

As I have suggested earlier, the United States possesses, to an even greater extent than she did in the early days of NATO, the power to dictate the military policy of the Alliance, even in the nonnuclear field. But if she exercises this power to the full, she runs two grave risks. The first is that of incurring the concealed resentment of European governments and public opinion. Europeans cannot but admit the prowess of the United States in military technology, but they are not prepared to accord her hegemony in the realm of ideas. And to create such tensions could militate against the true interests of the United States, since she is increasingly dependent on the political support of her European partners.

In the second place, it multiplies the effect of mistakes in American policy and increases the difficulty of correcting them. This will, I think, emerge clearly when it is possible to write the inner history of military policy in the Alliance during the last five or six years. American policy between 1954 and 1959 placed a decisive emphasis on firepower as compared with manpower, and the American Government persuaded its NATO allies of the importance of low-yield nuclear weapons and medium-range missiles to the defense of Europe. This policy was accepted by the European allies at first with misgivings, but later with enthusiasm as they became aware that this would largely relieve them of the need to increase their mobilized manpower. Then American views began to change, but since the allies had only a very fragmentary picture—through occasional briefings in the NATO Council, or in the ineffective Military Representatives' Committee in Washington—of the considerations that were causing American policy-makers to revise their view, they continued to apply the lesson they had learned so well. The consequence is that the British, German, and French military staffs are still much more enthusiastic about the use of low-yield nuclear weapons as part of their normal firepower than the American Army, which is abandoning the pentomic division and is trying to evolve a tactical doctrine that places less emphasis on tactical nuclear weapons.

It seems to me that it is in the interest of the United States to avert this kind of cleavage between herself and her NATO Allies (which has been muted but not healed by the Berlin crisis) and to shorten the time lag in conforming to modifications in military concepts (of which she must clearly be the fountainhead since her technology has so profound an effect upon them). The best way to do this would be to ensure that the Allies had continuous access to the inner debate from which American military policy emerges, and that they were accorded greater candor in discussions concerning American weapons developments. In other words, all her NATO Allies should now be on the same footing—as far as exchange of confidential information and views are concerned—as Britain and Canada have been since before NATO was founded. If the military policy of all the Allies for the defense of Europe is to respond to and keep up with technological development and events in the outside world, there is no alterative to a system of joint international planning in which the United States has a powerful but not overweening influence.

The obvious answer is that such a system exists already. All NATO commands, including the two Supreme Commands that play such an important part in the planning process, are international, although their commanders are American. They report to the Standing Group—that is, to the representatives of the United States, British, and French Chiefs of Staff in Washington, which in turn reports to the Military Committee, which consists of the Chiefs of Staffs of the Alliance. Their recommendations and modifications to each five-year plan then go before the NATO Council for approval. In theory, all military planning in NATO is internationally formulated, and does not go into effect until it receives the unanimous assent of the highest civil authority in the Alliance and of the member governments that it represents.

But significant differences have developed between theory and practice. For one thing, the Standing Group in Washington has become a somewhat shadowy organization with little influence either in the Pentagon or in the Alliance as a whole. SHAPE has become the dynamic center of military planning and since it is only twelve miles from NATO (while the Standing Group and the representatives of the Military Committee are 3,000 miles away), the Supreme Commander Europe has in reality become the Chief of Staff of the Alliance. With a man of such remarkable qualities as General Norstad, who was Supreme Commander from 1956 until 1962, this situation was, on the whole, acceptable. But even during his six years at SHAPE, certain weaknesses became apparent which are likely to become glaring as less gifted soldier-diplomats succeed him.

One is that it imposes a great strain on one man to function as a planner, as a military adviser to an international organization, and as a potential commander of so vast an area as NATO Europe. Another is that, as a planning headquarters, SHAPE tends to fall between two stools. Its director is an American, but as an international commander his views do not necessarily represent those of the U.S. Government. When, in November, 1960, General Norstad made public his views on the desirability of stationing MRBM's in Europe, he was widely thought, throughout Europe and the rest of the world, to be voicing a new American policy, when in fact he was attempting to speak only in his international role. Thus there is a danger that new ideas emanating from the NATO military staffs may be suspect in Europe because they look as if they were dictated in America, and equally suspect in Washington because they have not been through the American policy-making process.

But there are two more serious defects in the NATO planning process. One is that the formulation of military policy takes place entirely within military channels, and the military and civil channels meet only at the highest level, where it is hard to effect modifications. This is not to cast any doubt on the ability and integrity of NATO military staffs or on military planning as such. But as weapons become more lethal and more costly, as manpower and military budgets rise, and as research and development becomes more complex, the area of purely military consideration diminishes, and the diplomatic, arms-control, or economic aspects of military choices become more important. It is for this reason that foreign offices and treasuries have become so deeply involved in problems that even a decade ago were considered within the exclusive competence of chiefs of staff. It is also one reason why ministers of defense, who are a constitutional innovation of the last twenty years in all the NATO countries, have become such important political figures. To continue to plan through purely military staffs on the international level now contradicts national practice. Since it is far easier to reconcile the sometimes conflicting requirements of political stability and military defense when planning is in its formative stages, the case is strong for a joint civil-military staff or for welding the stronger civil secretariat we have envisaged for NATO with the existing military machine.

The other weakness is that American legislation and practice preclude the discussion by American officials with their fellow members of international staffs (except the British) of any plans that involve the use of nuclear weapons. In effect, every NATO staff has an American wing in which a number of highly important papers circulate which may be seen only by American eyes. No one wishes to prejudice security, but the upshot of this has been that other governments have had only a very cloudy impression of American dispositions in Europe in so far as nuclear weapons are concerned, of the purpose they are designed to serve, or of the action the United States would take in an emergency. In so far as the British are more closely in the American confidence than other countries, this serves to accentuate the sense of division between the Anglo-Saxon and the Continental halves of the Alliance, and in any case can hardly survive Britain's entry into a closer political relationship with Europe. Bilateral agreements, such as have been made by the United States with other countries to inform them about certain aspects of nuclear technology or tactics with which they may be especially concerned, are not adequate to give the sense of participation in the evolution of NATO policy as a whole that is so clearly needed to increase transatlantic confidence. It is true that security is an important consideration, but in view of the publicity that inevitably attends so much Western planning and development, it is only one consideration among several to be weighed. The fact that American senior officers in NATO have of late felt it necessary to stretch their instructions to the limit, in order to give their colleagues and associates in NATO a clearer picture of American dispositions and policy, is a recognition of this. The time, however, has come to change the instructions.

To summarize this aspect of the problem: With the demise of the strategy of "massive retaliation," the American conception of the requirement of the defense of Europe has markedly altered. Since American military power, both strategic and tactical, is decisive for the security of Europe, the NATO Allies must pay close attention to these changes. But it is politically most unwise for the United States to assume either that when she changes her policies her allies will respond only after long delay and much public friction, or that she can dictate military policy to them, even if the new policy offers them much greater security. However, without better access to the American policy-making process, how can the Allies keep in close touch with the factors that make it necessary to modify American policy, and justify to their own countries their own consequential actions? The European allies are neither cowardly nor stupid, even if they may be somewhat self-centered, but they lack the grist for the kind of continuous policy debate that goes on in Washington, and they are without large staffs of their own. They need a clearer insight than they now get into the considerations that affect American decisions, especially if they must justify costly and unpopular decisions to their own parliaments and publics.

IV

I repeat, the existing machinery for the joint planning of European defense has developed certain weaknesses. SHAPE has acquired too important a place in it, which has forced the Supreme Commander into an equivocal role as both an international leader and as an official of the U.S. Government. The Allied military channels of planning and consultation have too little connection with political planning. And the inability of American officials to discuss the considerations that affect nuclear weapons gives to the European staffs and governments only a hazy conception of American over-all policy, which leads to unrealism or archaism in the policies and attitudes of the latter.* The Kennedy Administration is reported to be disappointed with the response of its allies to its proposals for strengthening the conventional defenses of Europe. But American practice over recent years must bear a large share of the blame.

Nor is this by any means a one-way exchange. Not only have the European Allies important contributions to make in the field of military technology, as the extent to which British, French, and Italian designs and inventions have been accepted by U.S. forces indicates; they could make a vital contribution in the realm of ideas, but only if they are adequately informed. American policy was largely tone-deaf to the views of its allies during the mid-1950's,

* My colleague Michael Howard has raised the very relevant question of how such a proposal to bring Allied governments and officials within the ambit of American strategic planning on the use and deployment of nuclear weapons might affect the prospects of arms-control agreements, such as the proposals to withhold certain types of nuclear weapons from Central Europe. The problem must be faced, and for my own part, I do not consider it impossible to solve. It is not a question of U.S. officials disclosing technical information that would enable a European nonnuclear power to become one, or indeed of any necessity to impart highly classified information (such as yields or targets) that might filter through the arms-control inspectorate into the adversaries' hands. At the same time, I doubt if the German or any other NATO government would accept the discrimination that geographical denuclearization would involve without having continued and closer access to the over-all policy of the Alliance and the United States.

when Mr. Dulles was at the State Department and Admiral Radford was Chairman of the Joint Chiefs of Staff, and also when European opinion was extremely ill-informed on the trends of strategy and weapons development. That the worst mistakes in American strategic policy—the decision to overemphasize nuclear firepower, to distribute low-yield weapons to the Allies, to continue primary reliance on the manned bomber—were made during that period was not perhaps mere chance.

If the considerations that I have outlined are valid, they point in one direction. If the NATO Council is to become a more effective and authoritative center for the coordination of national policies, the standing of its individual members must be enhanced and its Secretariat considerably strengthened. At the same time, internal developments within the Alliance make it difficult to create any executive committee or political directorate of the nominally or traditionally most influential member governments. If the military policy of the Alliance is to be the servant rather than the master of its political aims, and its formulation a unifying rather than divisive process, there must be closer liaison between political and military planning, and continuous and intimate access for the European Allies to the American policy-making process.

The time, therefore, has come, in my view, to consider a radical overhaul of the institutions and machinery of the Alliance along roughly the following lines:

1) The NATO Council should be retained in its present form with two changes: (a) Its members should be elevated in status from professional diplomats to those with political standing in their own countries. (b) The offices of Secretary-General and Chairman of the Council should be separated. Chairmanship of a body that operates on the unanimity rule is a full-time job, analogous to that of a prime minister in a cabinet government. In the case of NATO, the task requires a great deal of discreet contact with government officials at the highest level and many carefully formulated public statements. It must be performed by a figure who commands a

special degree of public and political confidence throughout the Alliance. It is the Chairman of the Council who should be the principal public spokesman of the Alliance.

2) The post of Secretary-General should be retained, but its functions should be transformed. The Secretary-General should be what his name implies, the senior official in the Alliance. The best national analogy is with a Permanent Under-Secretary of a government department in the British civil-service system (though he should not, I think, be British). He should be a man of powerful intellect and considerable experience, with a strong control over the official machinery. His task would be not so much to evolve policy as to draw together the threads of official planning and controversy so that his political masters can be presented with clear and intelligible choices. He would be a powerful but not a public figure.

3) Under the Secretary-General, there should be a single unified Secretariat responsible for both political and military planning. Under him should come three Deputy Secretaries-General: (a) for European affairs; (b) for extra-European affairs, including liaison with the other alliances, SEATO and CENTO (which means, in effect, keeping in close touch with the development of American, British, and French policies in the Middle and Far East); and (c) for economic affairs, dealing with the industrial and financial problems of infrastructure, burden-sharing and support costs, rationalization of national armaments programs, and related questions (this department would be concerned with the economics and finance of NATO itself rather than with the general economic problems of the Allies). Each of these deputies would have an international staff under him that would assume direct responsibility for the wide range of subjects and projects now dealt with by the most cumbrous mechanism imaginable—committees of fifteen governmental representatives, of which there are twenty-three in all.

4) On the military side, there should be a new appointment, the Chief of Staff of NATO, a senior military officer (preferably one who has held the highest military office in his own country)

who would be the apex of the military-planning machine. He would have the same privileges as a chief of staff in the British or American systems—that is, right of access not only to his immediate superior, the Secretary-General, but to the Chairman and individual members of the Council. He would have a strong international military staff, including three Deputy Chiefs of Staff, one from each of the major allies. The Chief of the NATO Staff would be the channel for the transmission of directives to the two Supreme Commanders, Europe and Atlantic. The Standing Group in Washington should then be disbanded and the Military Representatives' Committee there broken up, with its members becoming part of national delegations to or military advisers for their representative to the NATO Council. At the same time, SHAPE should become an operational rather than a planning headquarters. This would not imply a demotion for SACEUR, for in the era of missiles and sensitive early-warning systems, operational responsibility for an area stretching from the North Cape to Tabriz, in places only 50 miles deep, involving the forces of thirteen different countries, is quite enough for one man to handle, if indeed it is not already too much.

5) Such a reorganization would be designed to improve the efficiency of an alliance of governments, and the new Secretariat would not have supranational powers. It is, therefore, necessary to devise means for regular and effective national control of and agreement to the proposals of this powerful new staff. Otherwise, its work and authority would be undermined by national doubts and jealousies. To a large extent, this danger would be met by creating a more authoritative NATO Council, but there are still thorny problems that need continuous and expert review and resolution. It has long seemed to me that two short meetings of NATO foreign ministers a year (one of which includes finance and defense ministers) is inadequate for this purpose, since there is time only for the most general *tour d'horizon* at each meeting. What seems to be required is: (a) a quarterly or biannual meeting of defense ministers (whose increasing importance we have noted) and their

chiefs of staff, to review the work of the Military Planning Department of the Secretariat; (b) a biannual meeting of foreign ministers to review the work of the two political sections; and (c) an annual or biannual meeting of ministers of finance and trade (or industry) to review the work of the economic section. Clearly, these meetings could be made to overlap to give at least one general plenary session.

v

It is always a rash step for a layman to attempt to draw up even the most general and outline sketch for an official organization, and I can imagine a number of objections to this proposal for a single civil-military Secretariat under a strengthened Council.

The first is that to obliterate any formal distinctions among the various NATO powers—for instance, by abolishing the Standing Group, by lessening the importance of SACEUR, and by making the NATO Council the effective governing instrument of the Alliance—is to obscure the very different sizes, strengths, and resources of the various Allies. But, in fact, the shadow would be discarded for the substance, and the differing importance of the Allies more usefully registered, by the distribution of senior appointments in a more powerful working team. The following suggests one reasonable distribution of power and responsibilities:

Chairman of the Council: from a smaller European power

Secretary-General: from the United States

Deputy Secretaries-General

    a) for European affairs: from France

    b) for extra-European affairs: from the United Kingdom

    c) for economic affairs: from Germany

Chief of Staff: from the United States or the United Kingdom

Clearly, the attempt to create a more effective and unified machinery for the coordination of policy would fail if any of these different offices was regarded as the prerogative of a particular government, and if personalities, personal gifts, and personal experience were to play no part in the choice of the senior officials. However, it would be wise to establish certain fixed principles at the outset if this reorganization is to fulfill its aim. One is that the Secretary-General, with his revised responsibilities, should be an American (and of course a civilian). It is only by placing an American at a key point in the structure that the Alliance can rely upon continuous contact with the working bureaucracy in Washington. His function would be complementary to that of the American representative on the Council, whose job it is to act as an interpreter of American policy at the highest level. It is true that the American civil service and administrative system do not breed many men of the type required, but in other international organizations Americans have fulfilled a post of this kind with great success. A second principle is that the Deputy Secretaries-General should not be American. This is not suggested in order to satisfy British or French or German *amour propre*, but because of the importance, in terms of inter-Allied confidence, of interposing influential non-American voices in the political planning process. The Chief of Staff, however, probably should be an American, with British, French, and German Deputy Chiefs of Staff under him. Under them should come a fully integrated international military planning staff, to work on the kind of intricate problems discussed in the last chapter, so that the Council may have the raw material on which to base its decisions. The question of whether the Supreme Commander Europe should continue to be an American should be determined by the policies of Britain and France. The decision should not be determined solely by the fact that at present only an American can control the use of nuclear weapons, since this may eventually need modification. But, at the moment, the United States is making the greatest single contribution, direct and indirect, to the security of Europe. If this should change, if France were to assume a larger share of the burden and the position of French senior officers became less controversial than at present, the case for a French SACEUR would be a strong one, for the restoration of the defenses of Europe is a task which France is historically and geographically best suited to undertake.

The second objection to the idea of a combined civil-military Secretariat in NATO is that men of the caliber required to make it a really effective center of international planning would not be forthcoming—would not be made available by the member governments. Certainly, if this were true it would be a grave objection, for nothing is gained by creating a large second-rate bureaucracy at the heart of the Alliance. But this is a problem by no means confined to NATO, for it affects the relations of governments with the U.N., its specialized agencies, and other international organizations. The crucial point (which has been recognized in other spheres) is that the interests of a government may now be much better served by sending one of its best men to NATO than by retaining him within its own foreign office or ministry of defense. In considering men for the NATO Secretariat, which should be strong rather than large, governments should ask themselves if they can spare X: if the answer is yes, he should not be appointed; if the answer is no, then he is the right man. There is no doubt that if certain governments took the lead in sending men of high quality, the others would, in self protection, follow suit.

The third objection is that made by the military—namely, that in a combined organization of this kind, military considerations may be obscured or military advice may not be presented to the Council and to member governments with the clarity and detachment that are needed. This objection can be met in two ways. One is to acknowledge that it has some force, and to give to the Chief of Staff the right of access to the Council. The other is to remind military staffs that the field of purely military planning or of purely military considerations is diminishing all the time, and cannot be considered—if it ever could—in a political and economic vacuum without doing grave damage to the general objectives of the Alliance. In this sense, the reorganization would merely have the effect of bringing the practice within NATO into line with that of most of its member governments. With the development of ministries of defense over the last two decades, the purely military element in the machinery of defense planning has diminished in importance, and the evolution of national security policy—which in earlier peacetime periods was largely a matter of trilateral bargaining between the chief or chiefs of staff, the treasury, and the head of government—today involves continuous consultation between civilian and military planners at all levels and many departments. The time is overdue to make the formulation of international security policy follow the same pattern.

Then it can be asked whether a mere reorganization of the machinery of the Alliance would have a significant effect upon the problems that have been discussed earlier. Are not the spirit of the Alliance and the attitude of member governments toward their obligations of much greater importance? Until these change, would not a reorganization of the central institutions be an attempt to cure the symptoms rather than the cause of division and malaise?

With national governments, this is very often the case: Setting up the ministry of X or disbanding the ministry of Y rarely provides a solution to the real problem. But in the case of international organizations, this is not true. Structure may have a considerable bearing on the policy adopted, as Mr. Khrushchev clearly acknowledges when he demands a reorganization of the machinery of the United Nations. Moreover, in an alliance rather than a world organization, the adjustment of the central machinery can have a distinct bearing on the readiness of the member governments to accept and support the decisions and plans of the alliance as a whole, because they are better able to convince their own countries that they themselves have played an important part in shaping these decisions. In the case of NATO, it is no accident that the governments of some of the smaller countries are unwilling to defend or implement NATO policy, because it is only hazily understood by their officials and is regarded by their national public opinion as having been dictated by the United States. In the same way, the uncooperative role of France in NATO in the last few years is connected with the fact that the only senior appointment held by a Frenchman in the central machinery, membership in the Standing Group in Washington, has lost all real power or significance.

Finally, the most cogent objections to strengthening the central institutions of NATO are that it might tend to bureaucratize the already difficult process of arriving at national or international decisions on policy, slow down the reactions of the leading powers to developments in the rest of the world, and reduce policy decisions merely to inarticulate compromises between different national positions. To a certain extent, this problem is inherent in the existence of the Alliance itself, but I would argue that such a reorganization would minimize it, for two reasons. The first is that by giving the smaller Allies a more intimate working knowledge of the trends of British and American policy and contingency planning, it would, in fact, give the larger countries a freer hand to take swift political or military action in a crisis. The second is that by enhancing the status of the Council *and* creating a strong civil-military Secretariat, it would be possible to work for international decisions at the proper level. A more authoritative Council by itself would be insufficient, since busy political figures cannot be expected to spend the hours or weeks of discussion that are generally necessary to evolve constructive policies, whereas junior teams of officials can. Without a stronger Secretariat, the members of the Council would be apt merely to parrot standard national policies and attitudes instead of using the fruits of intelligent official debate within the Secretariat as the starting point of discussion. Without a stronger Council, much of the work of the Secretariat would go to waste, gathering dust in the archives of national governments.

This reorganization would, in my view, have a significant effect on the cohesion and effectiveness of the Alliance. But most important of all, no better relation of the Alliance as such to the actual control of nuclear weapons is conceivable without strengthening NATO's central institutions. I have suggested that if Britain and

France are prepared to accept the role of purely European nuclear powers, with their forces operating within a NATO plan, then the problem becomes less formidable. But conversely, NATO would have to be in a position to undertake such planning, to be an impressive and authoritative planning center, before the two countries would be prepared to relinquish their nuclear independence. And in my view, this authority can only be acquired with a high-grade civil-military staff operating under a strong Secretary-General and Chief of Staff, who are in turn responsible to a Council of enhanced standing.

The other aspect of nuclear control concerns tactical weapons. We know it is desirable, in terms of European stability and of Soviet confidence in NATO's ability to control its members and forces, that there should normally be as tight a system of safeguards on nuclear weapons in Europe as human wit can devise. But it is not certain that it will continue to be the wise course to insist that these weapons can be used on the authority of the President of the United States alone. There is a sound case for arguing that the Russians will be most effectively deterred from embarking on any adventure in Europe when they know that there is some other authority than the American President—against whom they can bring formidable strategic pressures to bear in a crisis—who can order that nuclear weapons be used against military forces attacking in Europe.

It seems highly undesirable that this authority should be a single military officer such as SACEUR, let alone any of his junior commanders. To devolve such power to the head of the government of the country under attack might have a disuniting effect on the Allies as a whole; and, if several countries were under simultaneous attack, it might be a source of military confusion. The soundest course might be to vest in the NATO Council itself the power to order the use of short-range, low-yield nuclear weapons on the recommendation of the Chief of Staff. It is true that the Council operates on the unanimity rule and does not take decisions by

majority vote, but so also do national cabinets on all matters of
real importance, and such a decision would only be required of
the Council if the danger was clear and unmistakable.

But two preconditions are essential if the Council is to acquire
an operational responsibility of this kind. First, it must have had
the opportunity to consider in advance and in detail, through its
staff, the kinds of circumstance in which it would authorize the use
of short-range tactical weapons—a Soviet attack with nuclear weapons, a Soviet conventional attack, an attack confined to one country, and many other permutations of circumstances. This argues
for a strong staff. The other precondition is that it have some standing in its own right, that men who represent different countries on
it have immediate access to their heads of government and be
deeply trusted by them. Only by this means can collective decisions be taken with the minimum delay for governmental consultation.

The only alternative, therefore, to the politically unacceptable
course of an American military domination of all command decisions in the Alliance is, in my view, to build up, in the manner
outlined, the authority of the Council and the effectiveness of the
combined staff.

VI

No discussion of the means for better coordination of policy
within NATO, or better balance and distribution of the over-all
force of which it disposes, has much reality without an examination
of the economic and logistic base on which such planning must
rest. These logistic arrangements have been evolved throughout
the life of the Alliance. They are complex, and they cover a wide
range of activities that include not only problems of common
financing for airfields and pipelines and of attempts to standardize
weapons, but also agreements on civil-emergency planning, the
stockpiling of raw materials, and air navigation. I am concerned
here with only two questions, both of which raise problems of in-

creasing magnitude. The first is whether the principle of common financing for installations that are used in common should be extended. The second is whether progress can be made in the standardization of weapons on an Atlantic basis or on that of a European-American partnership.

The achievements of the infrastructure program of common financing of projects that serve an Allied purpose have been very considerable. Over the eleven years that the program has been operating, some $3.4 billion has been allocated, under a cost-sharing formula that has been revised three times. It includes 220 serviceable airfields, 5,300 miles of pipeline, and 27,000 miles of signal communications. The European early-warning system is nearly complete, and in the last three years, the program has been. extended to cover such things as nuclear-weapons stores, air defense equipment, and missile sites. The number of projects, and inevitably their cost as well, that serve the needs of the Alliance as a whole rather than any one country is increasing. But infrastructure projects were formerly confined to items that are immovable: the pipeline, but not the tanker; the airfield, but not the aircraft; the missile site, but not the missile. The relevant question is whether the principle should now be extended beyond static installations in order to create a stronger incentive for Allied rather than purely national projects. The case for doing so is a strong one. In the first place, infrastructure is an equitable system, since where the money is spent is related to geographical and military considerations rather than to national ones.* In the second place, the more common projects of this kind there are in Europe, the greater is the authority of NATO and SACEUR on whose recommendation they are undertaken.

* The present division of infrastructure costs in percentages is as follows:

Belgium	4.24%	Luxembourg	0.17%
Canada	5.15%	Netherlands	3.83%
Denmark	2.87%	Norway	2.37%
France	12.00%	Portugal	0.28%
Germany	20.00%	Turkey	1.10%
Greece	0.67%	United Kingdom	10.50%
Italy	5.97%	United States	30.85%

The case against extending infrastructure is that it has a cumbersome procedure for arriving at decisions that is inevitable in an alliance of sovereign governments. As the system works at present, it sometimes takes as long as fifteen months to have a new project approved by the Standing Group and the fifteen-nation Infrastructure Committee of the Council. The country on whose territory the installation is to be built must then draw up the plans (with international competitive bidding) and have them unanimously approved. This has sometimes meant a lag of three to five years from the time when a project was first discussed to the time when it was actually completed—particularly if it needed any modification.

The reason for the cumbrousness of infrastructure programing does not arise merely from the fact that it requires consent at each stage from fifteen national representatives. (If it were this alone, it could be cured by the transition from a system of governmental committees to a genuine international staff.) It is partly due to the attitudes of governments and business and labor leaders, and to the fact that the concept of interdependence has never percolated down to the lower levels of national civil services. Until recently, some transitory factors also slowed down the process. One of the most obvious was that European engineering industries were heavily overloaded during the years of recovery; now, however, there is more spare engineering capacity in Europe. Though it seems probable that the more advanced technical projects—particularly for new weapons systems—will be developed primarily by the leading industrial countries in the Alliance, particularly the United States and Britain, there is much better hope of getting engineering projects fulfilled from European sources than there was during the early days of the infrastructure program.

There are some sound arguments against extending the infrastructure program beyond its present limits of about $280 million a year, even if its administrative procedure could be improved. For one thing, the present burden-sharing formula is based on the overall economic capability of each member country and not on its actual military effort, so that two countries of similar size, one of which is making twice the military contribution of the other, will be assessed on the same basis. With a relatively small program, such inequities may be bearable, but as Malcolm Hoag points out in one of the few scholarly analyses of the problem: "The gross arbitrariness of the formula becomes less acceptable as the total contributions rise."* However, the formula was successfully revised in 1960, and the share of the United States, which was originally 43.6 per cent, was reduced to 30.8 per cent, while the countries of the European Economic Community (including Britain) now shoulder about 55 per cent.

Another drawback is that NATO as such has no responsibility for the construction or actual ownership of hardware. The difficulty in taking a major step forward toward any principle of common ownership (as opposed to common financing of a facility or site whose actual ownership remains with the country on whose soil it is located) is that there is no traditional conception of temporary international ownership. Except for communications, where most of the fifteen nations use the same facilities in common—and where the principle of supranational ownership has, in fact, been applied empirically by making SHAPE into the host country— each of the other programs financed by infrastructure has not normally been used in common by more than a small proportion of the fifteen nations. But, as this decade advances, every missile site in Italy and every radar station in Norway will become as vital to the defense of Britain or of Canada as they are to Italy and Norway themselves. No one would wish to saddle NATO with large-scale ownership of the means of deterrence and defense, but the number of projects that serve an Atlantic—rather than a national or even regional—purpose is expanding so rapidly that there is a strong case for asking if the concept of common ownership cannot be broadened. The distinction that has confined such financing to fixed objects will slowly break down or lose all military significance as the installations or forces based on the soil of different European

* "On NATO Pooling," *World Politics*, April, 1958.

countries—mobile-based missiles, vertical take-off aircraft, warning, guidance, and antisubmarine systems—come to serve more and more a hemispheric and less a national function.

Nor should this problem be conceived only in terms of the more complex weapons systems. It is well worth considering whether the basic elements of a more mobile and effective ground force in Europe should not be internationalized in this fashion. The difficulties that have been experienced by the countries with troops in Germany—particularly Britain—in negotiating the question of "support costs" year by year, have left a nasty taste in the mouths of all concerned. If a mobile force is the true strategic requirement for the Central Area, there is a good case for arguing that such things as barracks, dumps, and stores should be taken out of the field of normal bilateral negotiation and be commonly financed— if not by the whole Alliance, at least by the eight nations committed in that sector.

Finally, there is the problem not only of equity but of incentives. Again, I quote Malcolm Hoag, one of the leading authorities in this field:

Discussing the impressive obstacles alone breeds a defeatism that no interest in equity for equity's sake can possibly overcome. It is the incentive aspect of a formal burden-sharing scheme that must be stressed. *The central dilemma of an alliance is that the more interdependent members become, the more the military efforts of allies are substitutable for effort of one's own.* [Italics added.] Hence the perverse incentive to slacken one's effort becomes greater. This effect is especially prominent for small powers. If doubling one's own military budget looks terribly costly, but can at best add only a little to the deterrent power of the Alliance, why do it? Apathy has been a grievous problem in NATO. It might be attacked by threats of withdrawing Alliance protection if greater effort is not forthcoming, e.g., "We would no longer propose to risk Chicago for Copenhagen." Obviously so drastic a means of attack is likely to over-shock those threatened from a state of apathy to one of angry despair. A far more subtle, although still forceful and politically troublesome, means of attack can be envisaged in the form of a burden-sharing scheme that provides for monetary transfers among members. To the extent a member then lags in its military program, it loses in claims for transfers from its allies or incurs increased transfer obligations to them. The finance minister may find himself more favorably inclined toward military programs in view of their new impact upon the balance of payments. This is strong medicine, and in the nature of the case neither the type of medicine nor its dosage would be perfectly appropriate. But it meets the inventive problem forcefully if imperfectly, and this great promise of a burden-sharing scheme must be balanced against its formidable technical and political difficulties.*

Whether any financial method can be devised and agreed upon which would provide effective incentives to the various countries to undertake projects that benefit the Alliance as a whole, I am not competent to judge. But what the layman can legitimately ask is whether it is possible to apply the principles of central banking to NATO, creating a small-scale version of the International Bank for Reconstruction and Development within the Alliance, so that a wider range of projects of common value could be commonly financed.

VII

The fifteen NATO powers spend nearly $70 billion on defense each year, of which probably some $50 billion is directly concerned with the defense of Europe and the NATO area. With such an enormous sum involved, it has always been a matter of speculation whether greater strength could not be produced at lower cost by some vigorous program for standardizing equipment both within Europe and between Europe and the United States, and for concentrating production in those countries where it was most economic. The subject has been a live one ever since NATO was founded, but it has recently become urgent, for three reasons.

In the first place, until a few years ago the United States was the supplier of all the major armaments in NATO except the small proportion supplied by the United Kingdom. There was, therefore,

* *Op. cit.*

in NATO, a rough *de facto* standardization on American equipment financed by American military aid. This is no longer true,
for there are now eight countries producing armaments within the
Alliance, and military aid has virtually ceased. In the second place,
the general recognition of the need to diversify the military strength
of the Alliance has coincided with various technological developments that are advancing steeply the costs of all forms of equipment—conventional or unconventional. Finally, the economic regeneration of Europe, coupled with high defense expenditures
throughout the Alliance, has created a very close connection between military policy, employment policy, and commercial interests. There can be no tidy blueprint for a better division of responsibility in this field, since on both sides of the Atlantic the
jobs of hundreds of thousands of men, the future of great en-
terprises, and the political standing of democratically elected governments are involved. For these reasons, it is very much easier to
talk about standardization of weapons and specialization on the
part of different countries than it is to achieve them, despite the
fact that the advantages of interdependence are most obvious in
this field.

Indeed, this last question has made the problem of interdependence in weapons and equipment much harder to solve in the last
few years. The United States is now running a steady balance-of-
payments deficit with Europe, of which the $1.5 billion she spends
on forces and equipment in Europe is a substantial factor. In the
last two years, she has tried to offset this by increasing her sale of
arms to Europe. This has had two immediate effects. The first is to
draw her into sharp competition with the United Kingdom, which
depends upon a regular sale of armaments to Europe, particularly
Germany, in order to finance her contribution to the NATO
forces there. It has also saddled NATO with certain types of American equipment that are not necessarily suitable to its needs. Unfortunately, the strength of American industrial groups combined
with the present sluggish state of the American economy have
made the United States Government most unwilling to contem-

plate leaving special kinds of weapons production to Europe or buying European products for the United States forces.

There are three stages in the fruition of any military product—whether it be a weapon, a uniform, or a radar system. The first is the operational requirement—namely, the military function that the weapon, vehicle, ship, and so forth, is designed to serve. It is hard enough to get agreement on, say, the right kind of tank or ship within a particular service in one country; and the problem can become formidable when transferred to the international scene. The reason is that national staffs have widely differing views, which the pressure of time and circumstance have not eliminated, on the tactical employment of a particular weapon. One striking example has been the medium tank, where the British requirement is for a heavily armored and gunned vehicle while the French and German requirement is for a lighter and faster one. As the defense of Europe comes to take a higher priority in the thinking of all national staffs in European NATO, this disagreement is being mitigated, and there are encouraging signs of closer cooperation between Britain and the Continental countries in the design of a new tank and other vehicles. But in terms of a true system of interdependence within NATO, there is only one technique that is really effective. This is to get NATO itself to lay down its own requirements. This has been done with success in one case—that of the G.91 Fiat light fighter—where the specification was laid down by SHAPE in default of agreement among the different nations on which of several national designs to adopt. However, a similar attempt to produce an agreed specification for a VTOL aircraft seems to have failed.

The second stage in the production of a weapon is the inevitably lengthy process of research and development that must precede any actual production order. This is essentially a job for commercial firms and government research establishments. NATO now has modest resources to stimulate lines of research in which, for one reason or another, no national government can be induced to take a sufficient interest.

The difficulty arises in the transition from research and development to actual production. The latter takes up a shorter part of the time that separates the establishment of the requirement from the actual equipment of the troops, but it is most profitable for the countries and firms that undertake it. It is not easy for NATO to award a development contract to one country or firm without awarding it the production order as well, even if the firm lacks the resources to produce the order as quickly and efficiently as the needs of the Alliance may require. Considerable progress has been made in dividing up production contracts—such as those for the F.104G Star-fighter, the Hawk missile, the Sidewinder air-to-air missile, or a maritime patrol aircraft—among various European countries under a single project management. This, however, has been done primarily with weapons designed in the United States, and has not always proved economical or speedy.

When the original edition of this book was written, the prospects for an interdependent Allied system of weapons production seemed brighter than they do today. On the one hand, the regeneration of European pride and skill makes it less and less palatable for European countries to accept any division of labor whereby research and development on advanced weapons systems is concentrated primarily in the United States and Britain. Clearly, Europe is going to have to think hard and long before deciding to attempt large missile systems, but, especially in the field of aircraft, European technical ambition will not easily be diverted. On the other hand, the prospect of the United States leaving research and development on conventional weapons primarily to advanced European countries seems ruled out for political and economic reasons. But an attempt by the United States to solve its balance-of-payments problems by the sale of arms to Europe could seriously distort NATO costs and planning, and create considerable friction within the Alliance.

On most aspects of NATO policy that have been discussed in this book, it has been suggested that the strategy and policy of the Alliance are indivisible. But in the field of development and production, my own belief is that it would be wiser to look to a different formula, whereby the European countries increasingly complement each other's efforts but do not attempt to achieve a significant degree of common production or standardization with the United States. Britain can accept the fact that, even though she still has important commitments in the Far East, her tanks must now be designed primarily for use in Europe by Europeans, for the simple reason that Europe has become her most important obligation. She can be expected to develop closer and closer relations with France, Italy, and Germany in this field. But, quite apart from the difficulty that American industry and bureaucracy have in accepting foreign equipment, American weapons must still be designed for a world-wide purpose, since she is the only true world power in the Alliance.

If it is a prime interest for Europe to develop its great resources of skill and power to produce standardized European weapons, it is also a prime European interest that the United States should remain militarily involved in Europe. If this continues to be a financial drain on American reserves of gold and foreign currency, it would seem to be advantageous for Europe to subsidize directly the costs of the American forces in Europe, perhaps through the kind of central banking technique I have suggested, rather than indirectly by the purchase of American weapons which may not suit their needs.

CONCLUSION

This book is by no means a comprehensive study of the development of NATO or of the contemporary political and military problems that confront the Alliance. It does not deal in any detail with the history of the Alliance, nor does it attempt to quantify the problems that will confront it in the next few years, in terms of money and material. But if it succeeds in conveying a broad picture of the kinds of pressures, both external and internal, to which NATO is now subjected, and in outlining some of the means by which the central core of the system could be strengthened, it will have served its purpose.

Though it deals with hard and difficult problems, it is not written in any negative spirit of fear that these pressures will disrupt or break NATO. Though it takes account of both the promise and limitations of the concept of Atlantic partnership between a strong United States and a daily-strengthening Europe, it is written in the conviction that, in the nuclear missile age, strategy and policy are indivisible.

These words of the present Secretary-General of NATO, Dr. Dirk Stikker, express my own sentiments as a European:

> It is perhaps understandable, too, that like the man in the Bible, having waxed fat, we should kick—in other words, that we should celebrate our new-found prosperity with a greater sense of independence from what some of us are inclined to see as the tutelage of the United States. It is a healthy enough sign in its way; but the trend goes too far when it becomes, as it sometimes does, an attempt to make of a united Europe a separate force which might ultimately and

in some way hold the balance between East and West. The concept of equal partnership in our alliance is one which I hold very dear. Nevertheless, I say this, and I say it with all the emphasis at my command: The defense of the free world is indivisible. Our liberties and our very lives depend on the closest possible partnership between those members of the alliance who live on this side of the Atlantic and those who live on its western shores. The Atlantic must unite and not divide us. A large part of my political life has been given to forwarding the cause of European unity. But I should feel that that cause had been betrayed if it could triumph only at the expense of weakening the Atlantic partnership in NATO on which, in the last resort, our whole future depends.*

* Copenhagen, September, 1962.

APPENDIX:
THE COMMUNIST BLOC AND
THE WESTERN ALLIANCES

The Military Balance, 1962-63

This is the fourth annual estimate compiled by the Institute for Strategic Studies of the nature and size of military forces of the groups of states involved in the Cold War—the Communist bloc (excluding Yugoslavia but including Albania,. which is still formally a member of the Warsaw Pact) and those countries with which the United States has mutual-defense treaties. The Institute assumes full responsibility for the facts and judgments which this estimate contains.

The estimate examines the military balance as it existed at the end of October, 1962, and as it will, on present indications, change during the ensuing year. No longer-range projections of force levels or weapons beyond 1963 have been included. Missiles of 600–1,000-mile range are all described as MRBM's (medium-range ballistic missiles).

Manpower figures given are those of regular forces, although an indication of the size of militia or of paramilitary forces has been given in the sections dealing with individual countries. Naval strengths are those of active fleets and ships in commission only, except where otherwise stated; ships of Western navies below 100 tons have been omitted.

The tabular material at the end should not be regarded as a comprehensive guide to the nature of the balance of strategic power since it does not reflect important advantages of geography, invulnerability of bases, efficiency, etc., on both sides. It may, however, be found useful in the context of discussions on disarmament, and of the general balance of power.

PART I. THE COMMUNIST POWERS

THE SOVIET UNION
(Population 218 million)

General

Throughout 1962 Soviet defence policy has pursued a course not dissimilar, with one major exception, to that of the United States. The emphasis on strategic nuclear weapons as the primary means of ensuring national security has been officially maintained, but increased emphasis has been placed on the modernization of the conventional land, sea (particularly submarine) and air forces, both tactical and interceptor air defence. Defence expenditure has been slightly increased; the projected reduction in Soviet military manpower has been further postponed; close attention has been given to the quality and training of the fighting forces; research and development on new aircraft, missiles and conventional weapons appears to have been accelerated; the nuclear submarine programme is beginning to gather momentum; the active defences of the Soviet Union have been strengthened and it has even been asserted that the problem of finding a defence against the missile has been mastered by the Soviet Union.

The essential difference between the Soviet and the American policies concerns strategic weapons. The development of a large number of different strategic weapons systems on the part of the United States, coupled with a doctrine of controlled *counter-force* strike as the first response in the event of general war, does not find a parallel in Soviet policy. It appears that the Soviet leaders have decided to concentrate on increasing the destructive power of their strategic striking force, as well as somewhat augmenting the number of units of delivery, by improving the ratio of weight-to-yield in the warheads of strategic missiles, and by emphasising, in their policy statements, the havoc that would be wrought on Western *cities* in a strategic exchange.

As Mr Khrushchev put it at the Moscow Peace Congress in July 1962, '. . . In order to ensure its security the Soviet Union has been forced in the last few years to create nuclear weapons of 50, 100 and more megatons, intercontinental rockets, a global rocket which practically eludes the defences, and an anti-missile rocket . . .' The main task of the armed forces, as described by the Defence Minister, Marshal Malinovsky, is 'to study and work out methods of combat operations in conditions of nuclear-missile warfare, methods of repelling an aggressor's sudden nuclear attack, and of frustrating his aggressive intentions by means of the timely infliction of a crushing blow on him.'

The Soviet Union thus appears committed to a policy of 'minimum' or counter-city deterrence in relation to the United States, though the large medium range missile force it has now developed and deployed against targets in Europe and Japan may serve as both a counter-city and a counter-force threat. The Soviet leaders have denied that they are undertaking a large scale civil defence shelter programme; in January 1962 Marshal Malinovsky described bomb shelters as 'nothing but a coffin': however, civil defence training continues.

In January 1960 it was announced that Soviet forces were to be reduced from 3,623,000 men to 2,423,000 men by the end of 1961, but this reduction was suspended in July 1961 after about 600,000 men had been demobilized, principally in the ground forces. Then it was announced in August 1961 that the demobilization of certain categories of other ranks, whose period of military service was completed, had been suspended until the signature of a German peace treaty. Thus, at the end of 1961, the size of the Soviet forces stood at about 3,800,000 men. But, in fact, this deferred class began to be released gradually in the spring of 1962, and in September 1962 it was announced that all would be released and the next age group (those born in 1943) would be called up. The total size of the Soviet forces therefore stood at about 3,600,000 in the autumn of 1962. The age for compulsory registration has now been lowered from 18 to 17, partly because the Soviet Union is feeling the effects of the low birth rate of the war years.

The Soviet military budget for 1962 (calendar year) was set at 13,400 million roubles ($14,740 million). This represents a rise of 44 per cent on the original figure for 1961 (9,255 million roubles), but this was augmented by one third in July 1961 to 12,400 million, so that the 1962 figure is only 8 per cent higher than the final figure of the previous year. In real terms, the total size of the present Soviet budget is estimated to be as much as $33,000 million. This increase indicates an acceleration of research and development into, and production of, advanced weapons systems.

Air and Missile Power

Soviet policy statements continue to place marked emphasis on the development of long and medium range missiles as a deterrent to aggression and a support to diplomacy. The Soviet Union could, if the programme had rated a high enough priority, have by now built up a force of several hundred ICBMs, the original three-stage liquid-fuelled missile which has been under development since the mid-fifties. The reasons why they have not created an operational force of this size appear to be:

(a) The fact that in the period 1958–60 Mr Khrushchev thought that he could ensure the security of the USSR economically through the provision of relatively small forces of intercontinental bombers, ICBMs and missile firing submarines, enabling him to devote more resources to non-military programmes;

(b) the difficulties of building multiple bases for so large a missile;

(c) the fact that they have had a smaller second generation ICBM under active development for two years which is likely to be easier to conceal;

(d) the admitted demands of the Soviet space and other programmes upon technical resources.

Consequently the present figure of operational ICBMs is in the neighbourhood of 75. However, these ICBMs have very powerful boosters and can carry larger warheads than their American equivalents such as *Titan*. In theory, at least, they have the lift to boost the 50-megaton warheads which have been tested, and perhaps even larger ones, into a ballistic trajectory, though short of intercontinental range.

Soviet policy places considerable emphasis on concealment of missile bases as a form of protection. But, now, probably as the result of improved Western detection methods, some ICBM sites are being hardened, and increasing attention is being paid to the development of invulnerable submarine-launched missiles. However, the fact that some missiles are grouped in clusters on one site suggests that Soviet policy places greater confidence in active defence against American missiles, in just the same way that active defence against the manned bomber – fighters and ground-to-air missiles – has priority over passive measures. If so, this would give point to the Soviet concentration, evidenced in the speeches of Mr Khrushchev and Marshal Malinovsky during the past year, on anti-missile defence systems. Mr Khrushchev laid great stress during 1962 on the Soviet development of a 'global rocket', that is, one that could be launched on a trajectory to circumvent Western warning and other active defence systems.

By contrast with the small number of ICBMs, the number of MRBMs has been augmenting steadily and has now reached a figure of about 700. These are deployed in sufficient numbers to deal with strategic and semi-tactical targets – such as fighter airfields – in Western Europe, including Britain, and in the Far East. It is likely that this build-up is continuing. It is clear that Soviet policy is to site them near the western, southern and eastern borders of the Soviet Union, on the Pacific coast and in Siberia. The strategic missile forces are organized as an autonomous arm of the service, which is now believed to be under the command of Marshal Biryuzov.

In spite of their concentration on rockets and ballistic missiles, the Russians have not neglected their Air Force, which comprises some 15,000 operational aircraft, organized into five major components, namely:

(1) the long-range strategic bomber force;

(2) the tactical, or front line, force which

includes fighters and tactical bombers;

(3) the fighter interceptor force of the Air Defence Command;

(4) the land-based fleet air arm;

(5) the air transport force.

The heavy bomber force has been kept at a considerably lower strength than that of the US Strategic Air Command, though the general lines of development, including stand-off bombs and missiles, are similar. On the other hand the Soviet Union has built up a very strong force of medium bombers suitable for use all over the Eurasian theatre and its coasts, and an efficient light bomber force. The following gives some indication of Soviet strength in this field.

(i) Strategic Striking Power
Missiles

(a) The principal operational ICBM is propelled by a three-stage liquid fuel engine and has an operational range of over 8,000 miles.

A second generation ICBM has been developed with a warhead of between one and five megatons. It is propelled by a storable liquid fuel and is smaller and probably more accurate than its predecessor. It may be expected to be deployed during 1963.

(b) In November 1961 the 1st Deputy C-in-C Rocket Forces, General Tolubko, spoke of the range of strategic rockets as being over 620 miles. Soviet MRBMs are believed to include vehicles with ranges from 700 to 1,100 miles, based on Soviet territory. But there is a larger MRBM with a two-stage liquid fuel engine which has a range of 2,100 statute miles.

Long-range and Medium Bombers

The Strategic Bomber Force consists mainly of the following aircraft:

(a) 70 turbo-prop *Bears** (TU 20); now able to carry two short-range air-to-ground missiles or one large winged missile.

120 4-jet *Bisons*; now able to carry a winged missile.

(b) 1,000 twin-jet medium bomber *Badgers*

---

*It should be made clear that the menagerie of names for Soviet aircraft is of NATO, not Soviet, origin.

(TU 16). The air force version has a single air-to-ground missile like the US *Hound Dog*.

The Naval Air Force, a part of which is attached to each of the four Soviet Fleets, consists of about 750 aircraft, including a strike force of *Badgers* with winged missiles for ship attack.

(c) Delta-wing 4-jet *Bounder*. This could be a replacement for *Bison*, if the Soviet Union decided that there was a requirement for a supersonic strategic bomber.

There is a twin-engined supersonic medium bomber *Blinder*, somewhat similar to the US B58, coming into service with a long-range air-to-ground missile and probably capable of air refuelling. This is probably a replacement for *Badger*.

LRAF is grouped in three areas: Western Russia, the Central Ukraine and in the Far East, although it is likely that airfields in the Arctic are maintained for training and staging purposes.

(ii) Tactical Air Power

The tactical bomber forces are emerging from a period of transition with older aircraft such as the turbo-jet *Beagle* being replaced. The earlier estimate of 4,000 operational aircraft is therefore now too high. Priority now seems to be concentrated on a new twin-jet ground attack aircraft with transonic capabilities and a range of 2,000 miles which seems to be an improved version of *Flashlight* and known as *Flashlight B*. In general, intensive development work is going on in the field of supersonic high and low level attack bombers.

(iii) Air Defence

The number of ground-to-air guided missiles and high-performance fighters for air defence has been steadily increased and an extensive early warning system is in operation. The following are details of air defence equipment:

Ground-to-Air Guided Missiles

A radar-directed rocket, which is already in service and is considered to be highly effective. It is propelled by one main and one auxiliary solid fuel engine. Its slant range is

20 miles, and it rises to a height of at least 12 miles (60,000 feet).

There may also be a high-altitude guided missile, and there is an anti-aircraft missile which has a range of 18 miles.

A great deal of effort has been expended in the past year on the strengthening of anti-aircraft defences. In February 1962 Marshal Malinovsky said, '. . . The country's anti-aircraft defence troops have at their disposal weapons capable of destroying the aviation and outer space means of attack of the enemy at enormous distances and altitudes . . .'

Fighters

It is estimated that there are about 10,000 fighter aircraft of all kinds, and that intensive research and development to produce types with higher ceilings and improved air-to-air weapons has a high priority. Five types of air-to-air missiles have been displayed.

(*a*) The standard all-weather interceptor of recent years, the subsonic Yak 25 *Flashlight*, is now obsolescent, although two improved versions, one of them redesigned as a light bomber, are still in service. However, a new all-weather delta-winged interceptor, provisionally called *Flashlight C*, was displayed in July 1961. *Fiddler* is an all-weather long-range interceptor.

(*b*) The most important day fighters are:

	Maximum speed	Ceiling
	m.p.h.	feet
MIG 19 *Farmer*	900	55,000
MIG 21 *Faceplate*	1,200	60,000
SU 15 *Fishpot*	1,300	60,000+
SU 16 *Fishbed*	1,300	Rocket boosted

There are 600,000 men in the Soviet Air Forces.

Land Power

No official figures of the Soviet Army are published but its current total size is estimated at up to 2,500,000. It is organized in approximately 160 active line divisions, most of which are below full strength. Of this 160, about 75 divisions are in European

Russia and 26 in Eastern Europe. 20 are armoured divisions, 50 are infantry divisions, while the remaining 90 are in process of being converted into motorized divisions.

In East Germany there are 10 tank divisions each with 345 tanks, and 10 motorized divisions, each with 219 tanks. All are operational and comprise a total of over 5,500 tanks. In Hungary there are 4 divisions and in Poland 2 divisions. It is estimated that the Soviet Union has a total mobilization potential of 7 million men including all types of reservists.

A motorized division at war strength comprises nearly 14,500 men, a tank division about 11,250; both include supporting artillery and anti-aircraft units. There are still some rifle (infantry) divisions in the Soviet Union, but these are gradually being phased out.

The airborne forces of the Soviet Union total approximately 100,000 men formed in 9 divisions. The airborne troops are supported by the transport fleet, which would enable about two divisions to be air-lifted simultaneously.

In recent years, the Soviet Army has undergone a major reorganization to meet conditions of atomic warfare. Many of its units have been completely re-equipped twice over the last ten years and, thanks to the introduction of modern weapons, its fire power has been vastly increased. The large-scale introduction of tactical missiles into the Ground Forces has increased the importance of the former Artillery Command, which has been re-named the Command of Missile and Artillery Troops, and is under Chief Marshal of Artillery S. S. Varentsov. The main emphasis in training continues to be the movement of tank and missile-artillery formations across radiation-contaminated ground (including water and other natural barriers), consistent with Soviet doctrine which envisages a major offensive role for the Ground Forces in the event of nuclear war. Though the Soviet Union has not shown as much interest as the United States in the development of very low yield nuclear weapons for tactical purposes, nuclear warheads are available for many of the missiles mentioned below. The Soviet forces in East Germany have tactical nuclear weapons.

Soviet Army equipment includes:

(i) Tanks

The total strength of the Soviet Army is estimated at 20,000 front-line tanks and 15,000 second-line tanks. The new tanks which have been introduced into the Soviet armoured divisions are the T.54 medium tank fitted with a 100 mm. gun, and the 54-ton heavy tank T.10 which mounts a 122 mm. gun.

(ii) Artillery

The Soviet Army is very strong in artillery. Conventional weapons known to be deployed in field formations include cannon of up to 152 mm. calibre and unguided rockets of up to 240 mm. calibre, both with ranges of up to 13 miles, and short range mortars of up to 160 mm. calibre. Larger weapons exist which could have a nuclear capability but these are not known to be in field formations.

(iii) Missiles

Tactical missiles for use by the Ground Forces include those with ranges from 10 to about 300 miles, some of which are carried on modified tank chassis. The smaller missiles are all on amphibious tracked chassis.

Sea Power

The Soviet Navy, which is manned by about 500,000 officers and men (including the naval air force), has increased from a total tonnage in 1940 of 600,000 to 1,600,000 tons today, which makes it the most powerful fleet in the world after the United States (4 million tons).

(i) Submarines

The main strength of the Soviet Navy lies in the submarine fleet.

The submarine force comprises 410 units, of which 80 are based in the Baltic, 60 in the Black Sea, 130 in the Arctic, 120 in the Far East.

The number of conventional submarines has been reduced by 50 in the last three years. It is expected that, in the near future, 75 per cent of the submarine fleet will consist of ocean-going craft.

In October 1962 there were 10 nuclear powered submarines designed for various duties and in various stages of commissioning. The rate of building suggests that there may be between 15 and 20 by the end of 1963.

The following are details of the conventionally powered submarine fleet:

The F class is about 300 feet long, has a displacement of 2,000 tons, and a large radius of action. At least 10 of these are in service.

The G class is 310 feet long and has a submerged displacement of 2,700 tons. It has a very large conning tower for the vertical launching of missiles which are fired when on the surface.

The W class is 245 feet long with a 1,050 tons displacement. It has a speed of 16 knots on the surface and 13 knots submerged, and a radius of action of 10,000 miles. There are about 130 of these in service.

The Z class is 290 feet long with a submerged displacement of 2,600 tons. It is capable of 20 knots on the surface and 13 knots submerged, with a radius in excess of 20,000 miles. There are at least 20 of these in service. A small number have been converted to fire missiles, probably in a manner similar to the G class. They are stationed principally in the Baltic and the Far East.

The K and Q type, which were built between 1945 and 1955, are medium range vessels; their radius of action is about 7,000 miles and their displacement varies from 1,400 to 680 tons.

(ii) Surface Ships

The surface ships of the Soviet Navy consist of:

Cruisers	20
Destroyers	100
Guided Missile Destroyers	7
Other vessels	2,500

(There are also a number of disguised trawlers used for radar and reconnaissance purposes.)

These are distributed more or less equally between the Baltic, Black Sea, Northern and Pacific fleets.

The cruisers are of three different types:

(*a*) 14 *Sverdlov* class, launched between 1951 and 1957, displacement 15,500 tons, speed 34 knots, armament 12 152 mm. guns and 32 anti-aircraft guns;

(*b*) 3 *Chapayev* class, completed between 1948 and 1951, of 11,500 tons displacement, with the same speed and armament as the *Sverdlov*;

(*c*) 3 *Kirov* class, launched between 1936 and 1945, displacement 8,500 tons, speed 30 knots, armament 9 180 mm. guns and 20 anti-aircraft guns.

Four or more almost completed *Sverdlov* cruisers appear to have been scrapped.

The greater part of the destroyers are modern, having been constructed since 1950, and some are fitted with guided missiles. Their displacement varies from 1,000 to 2,700 tons, and their speed from 28 to 38 knots.

(iii) Fleet Air Arm

There are no aircraft carriers in the Soviet Navy, but there is a land-based Fleet Air Arm with 750 aircraft. It consists mainly of:

(*a*) the TU 16 *Badger* – range of 3,500 miles;

(*b*) the torpedo-carrying IL 28 *Beagle*, with a range of 1,500–1,800 miles;

(*c*) the older TU 14 *Bosun*.

A new twin-jet swept-wing flying boat *Mallow* (Be-8) intended for mine laying, and a naval turbine helicopter with a short-range missile were displayed in 1961.

(iv) Sea-to-ground Missiles

Since the series of Soviet nuclear tests in the Arctic in July 1962, there is no reason to dispute earlier Soviet claims that a true *Polaris*-type missile, which can be fired from a submerged submarine, has been successfully developed. Hitherto there have been two types. One has a range of about 100 miles and the other of about 400 miles. The 100 miles range missile is believed to be solid fuelled and can be fired either from a surface craft or a surfaced submarine. The 400-mile missile is designed for submarines but can only be fired from the surface.

THE WARSAW PACT NATIONS

It is estimated that the seven smaller members of the Warsaw Pact, whose organizational structure was tightened up during 1962, can muster about 63 regular divisions. These satellites' armed forces represent a total of about 980,000 men under arms (a small decrease over 1961). In addition there are about 285,000 men in para-military formations, (a decrease of over 25 per cent compared with recent years).

The table at the foot of this page gives the estimated strength of their armed forces.

The satellite air forces number a total of about 3,000 planes, about 80 per cent of which are jet fighters.

The satellite naval forces are of little importance and only of value for local defence.

THE WARSAW PACT FORCES

Country	Army	Navy	Air Force	Total Armed Forces	Para-Military	No. of Divisions	Destroyers	Sub-marines
East Germany	65,000	11,000	9,000	85,000	60,000	6	4	—
Czecho-slovakia ..	150,000	—	35,000	185,000	35,000	14	—	—
Albania	25,000	3,000	1,500	29,500	10,000	5 brigades	—	4
Bulgaria	100,000	5,000	15,000	120,000	40,000	10	3	3
Poland	200,000	12,000	45,000	257,000	45,000	14	3	7
Roumania	200,000	7,000	15,000	222,000	60,000	13	3	2
Hungary	75,000	—	5,500	80,500	35,000	4	—	—

CHINA

The Army

(*i*) The Army consists of well over 2,000,000 men organized in approximately 115 divisions of infantry; 2 or 3 armoured divisions; 1 or 2 airborne divisions; supporting troops; and cavalry for desert areas.

There were 125,000,000 men of military age in 1962. About 700,000 are called up each year and serve three years in the Army.

It is believed that a significant number of the best equipped and trained infantry divisions have been moved in the last year to Central and Southern China, opposite the Formosa Straits.

(*ii*) The armed forces are organized by the Ministry of Defence, advised by a National Defence Council whose Chairman is the Chairman of the People's Republic: control is exercised through 13 Military Regions. The Land Army consists of about 30–35 armies. These are of 3 divisions each, i.e. an Army is equivalent to a Western Army Corps. In peacetime there is no operational headquarters higher than the Army; but in wartime Armies are grouped in Field Armies. The strength of an active Army could be between 50,000–60,000.

(*iii*) No reliable figures are available for the size of the Militia, but the declared intention is to embody every third person in the population. Chinese policy places great emphasis on the militia, Mao's 'every man a soldier', but it is static, sketchily armed, and organized as much for forced labour as defence. The Public Security forces, including the armed police, now consist of about 300,000 men.

The Air Force

This has a total strength of 90,000 men and 3,000 aircraft, including 500 naval aircraft. China is now building jet fighters and trainers, but the backbone of the force consists of Soviet Mig 15s, 17s and probably 19s, IL 28 (*Beagle*) light bombers and helicopters. Mig 15s and perhaps 17s also are in quantity production in China. Training is inhibited by shortage of aviation spirit. A radar chain has been built along the Pacific coast from Kamchatka south to Hainan.

The Navy

China has no operational ships heavier than destroyers, of which there are 4. There are 30 submarines (a small increase on 1961), of which half are Soviet W class medium-range craft; frigates; MTBs; gunboats and patrol craft. The Navy is not an offensive force and is ineffective except for inshore defence.

NORTH KOREA

The Soviet Union concluded a mutual defence treaty with North Korea on July 7, 1961. The North Korean forces are estimated at 338,000 men, including an air force of 30,000 men and 500 planes; and an army of 16 divisions.

NORTH VIETNAM

Both the Soviet Union and China assist in the support of a conscript army which is estimated at 260,000 men organized in about 15 divisions. There are also 100,000 men in para-military formations.

CUBA

Cuba must, for the time being, be regarded as part of the Communist bloc. In the past two years the Cuban army appears to have been expanded from a regular force of about 30,000 to one of 80,000 equipped with recent Soviet weapons, and a militia of 200,000 men and women. There is an air force of about 70 Mig 17s and 19s, with some IL-14 transports: some IL-28 *Beagles* (subsonic 1,500-mile range, 4,000-lb bomb load) have also been supplied. It is clear that a strong force of surface-to-air missiles has been deployed. The Navy consists of 4 old cruisers and up to 20 modern Soviet motor torpedo boats. Many Cuban units now appear to be under Soviet command.

PART II.

THE WESTERN ALLIANCES

STRATEGIC FORCES

All strategic nuclear forces are under national control except for the NATO Striking Fleet Atlantic and the NATO Striking Force South which are called the US Second and Sixth Fleets respectively. An essential component of the strategic forces of the West is its air and missile warning systems.

(1) United States Air and Missile Bases

The United States has seven separate strategic weapon systems, and during 1962 rapid progress was made in the build-up and deployment of her missile systems. The US Secretary of Defense has claimed that the American strategic forces could still carry out devastating counter-attack on the centres of Soviet military power, even after absorbing the full impact of a Soviet first strike. Nevertheless strenuous efforts are being made to enlarge the size of the American strategic retaliatory systems and to make them less vulnerable to surprise attack. This is partly with a view to retaining the option of using the deterrent in a controlled and selective fashion in response to any local Soviet aggression.

Strategic Air Command is divided into:

(a) The Second, Fifth and Eighth Air Forces and the First Missile Division, all based on the continental USA.

(b) The Sixteenth Air Force in Spain, the Seventh Air Division in the UK, and the Third Air Division based on Guam.

Strategic Aircraft. By the beginning of 1963 the B-52 force should have expanded to the planned ceiling of 630 planes in 14 wings all based on the continental United States. Some will still carry only multi-megaton free falling bombs, but the B52-Gs (which have been in service for a year) carry – alter-

natively or additionally – two apiece of the *Hound Dog* missiles which can deliver 4-megaton warheads over 600 miles. The *Skybolt* 1,000-mile missile for the B-52H will not be in service in 1963.

The phased reduction of the B-47 medium bomber force, which was halted in 1961 at a level of 850 operational aircraft, is being resumed. Two wings of B-58 aircraft, with 45 aircraft in each, will be in position by December 1962.

About 600 KC-135 aerial tankers are in service extending the ranges of the bombers by in-flight refuelling.

The practice of maintaining 50 per cent of SAC aircraft on a 15-minute 'ground alert' is being continued.

Missiles. About 90 *Atlas* missiles are operational; within a year the number should rise to 126; the first 66 missiles are on 'soft' sites, but the remainder are to be deployed in 'hardened' sites. 36 *Titan* I missiles are in service now and another 18 can be expected by the end of 1962. 36 *Titan* IIs, which can be fired from underground silos, will become operational during 1963 and early 1964. 150 *Minuteman* missiles will be deployed in hardened silos by the end of 1962. Funds have been voted for a total of 800 *Minuteman*, of which 450 are planned to be deployed by July, 1963.

(2) RAF Bomber Command

This force includes about 180 *Vulcan*, *Victor* and *Valiant* bombers each able to deliver one or more multimegaton free falling bombs. It is trained and organized either to carry out strategic strikes in conjunction with or independently of United States strategic forces or to reinforce RAF overseas commands if a conventional or tactical nuclear war threat develops.

A number of squadrons have already converted to *Vulcan* B2, and will convert to *Victor* B2; both can carry the *Blue Steel* stand-off bomb. This missile, which flies with a thermonuclear warhead, is now becoming operational. As the planes to carry it are being acquired the *Valiants* are being increasingly employed as aerial tankers. About 100 *Valiants* are still flying in various roles.

Bomber Command keeps a proportion of its planes on ground alert.

Bomber Command also maintains 60 *Thor* missiles. The warheads are under Anglo-American dual control. These *Thors* are due to be scrapped by October 1963.

(3) The French Striking Force

A Strategic Air Command has been formed and is at present equipped with 40 *Vautour* IIBs capable of delivering high explosive bombs. This command will eventually have 50 *Mirage* IV light bombers capable of delivering the nuclear fission bombs that will then be available and supported by 12 KC-135 aerial tankers. The first seven *Mirages* are due to be delivered in 1963.

(4) European Missile Bases

The Italian and Turkish Air Forces maintain 2 and 1 squadrons respectively of *Jupiter* MRBMs. There are 15 missiles per squadron. In both cases the warheads remain under American control.

(5) Seapower

A high percentage of the 2,000 planes which can be embarked on the 21 attack carriers of the United States Navy could make a thermonuclear strike, but nearly half are designed primarily for air defence and would presumably be used in that role in general war. The most important attack plane (numerically) is the A4D *Skyhawk*, about 1,500 of which are flying with the United States Navy and Marine Corps. About 150 A3D *Skywarriors* are also in service and the first A3J *Vigilantes* are now being introduced.

9 *Polaris* ballistic nuclear-powered submarines have been commissioned and the figure is expected to rise to 18 by the end of 1963. Each boat is armed with 16 missiles. The first 6 were given the A1 *Polaris* which has a range of 1,200 nautical miles but the next 13 are being given the A2 which can travel 1,500 nautical miles. Unlike the carriers each of which is organic to one of the main USN fleets, these submarines form a separate command.

The British Fleet Air Arm now has 2 squadrons of *Buccaneer* aircraft in service. These can fly off carriers to deliver a thermonuclear bomb.

(6) NORAD

This command was formed through the integration of the Canadian and American air defences. It includes 5 Canadian interceptor squadrons whose CF-100 aircraft have now been almost entirely replaced by 66 F-101s.

The United States Air Defense Command has 1,500 fighters of which 500 are manned by the Air National Guard. They include some 400 F-101s, 700 F-102s and about 250 F-106s: the F-101s and F-106s have air-to-air missiles with nuclear warheads. Some F-86s and F-89s still in service will soon be withdrawn. The ADC also operates a considerable number of *Bomarc* ground-to-air missiles. Of these 180 are *Bomarc* As with a range of 250 miles and by July 1963 they will be supported by about 150 *Bomarc* Bs with a 440 mile range. The RCAF will man 2 *Bomarc* B squadrons with 28 missiles apiece.

The United States Army contribution to NORAD consists of the *Nike* series of ground-to-air missiles of which there are 12 launchers in a battery. The *Nike-Ajax* has an HE warhead and a slant range of 20 miles whereas the *Nike-Hercules* has a 75 mile slant range and offers the option of a nuclear warhead. In January 1962 76 *Nike-Ajax* batteries were still being manned by National Guard units but these are steadily converting to the *Hercules*. About 100 *Hercules* batteries have been established so far.

The Distant Early Warning line is the northernmost and most important of three lines of radar stations intended to track incoming manned aircraft. Airborne and seaborne stations constitute similar chains on the flanks of the DEW line and down the Central Pacific. Additionally 2 Ballistic Missile Early Warning Systems stations are in operation in Greenland and Alaska.

A complementary one at Fylingdales in Yorkshire should become operational by mid-1963. It will be used for tracking rather than detection. The BMEWS detection sets already in use can give S A C the necessary 15-minute warning.

NORTH ATLANTIC TREATY ORGANIZATION

There are three major military commands in N A T O – those of Europe, the Atlantic, and the Channel respectively. Of these only Allied Command Europe has national forces 'assigned' to its operational control in peacetime. However all three commands include 'earmarked' forces which are forces that member countries have agreed to place at the disposal of the commanders in the event of war. Other forces remain under national control either to ensure the defence of the national territories or to meet commitments outside the N A T O area.

The deployment of tactical nuclear weapons into N A T O land forces is continuing. The principal ones involved are *Honest John* at brigade or divisional levels and *Corporal* and *Redstone* at corps or army levels. The United States is the only country that has produced any nuclear warheads appropriate for missile delivery and she retains control over them even when the missiles themselves are operated by other national forces. Under the 'double-key' arrangements the nuclear warheads can only be fired by the mutual agreement of the USA and the host country. During 1963 *Pershing* and *Sergeant* will partially replace *Redstone* and *Corporal* respectively in the United States Seventh Army and *Pershing* will be acquired also by the Bundeswehr. The Seventh Army have introduced *Davy Crockett* mortars, which can throw a nuclear or high explosive shell 2–4,000 yards, down to the level of armoured reconnaissance companies but it appears that atomic warheads are retained at a higher echelon.

The N A T O infrastructure programme in Europe has been responsible for the development of 220 standard N A T O airfields capable of all-weather operation of all types of aircraft. They constitute the chief bases for the 5,500 or so tactical aircraft belonging to the air forces in Europe of the N A T O powers. Other major infrastructure achievements include the building of 5,300 miles of fuel pipelines together with storage tanks for 160,000 tons and the construction of 27,000 miles of communications and signals networks.

Certain pieces of equipment have been designated as standard for N A T O although this does not mean that they have been, or are intended to be, introduced into all national forces. The major weapon systems concerned include the *Hawk* and *Sidewinder* anti-aircraft missiles, the *Bullpup* guided bomb, the F-104G *Starfighter* and Fiat G.91 fighters, and the Breguet 1150 *Atlantique* maritime patrol aircraft. Multilateral production programmes for each of these systems have been initiated by various groups of N A T O countries. The most important of these is the F-104G *Starfighter*. It is intended to produce 233 by the end of 1962 and another 716 over the following 3 years. Of the total 604 are to go to Germany, 125 to Italy, 120 to the Netherlands, and 100 to Belgium. Canada is independently producing 200 for its own forces and 150 for Greece and Turkey. In addition Denmark will receive 40 F104s, and Norway 20, from the United States.

(1) Allied Command Europe

This has its headquarters near Paris and it covers the land area extending from the North Cape to the eastern border of Turkey excluding the United Kingdom, the defence of which is a national responsibility, and Portugal which falls under Allied Command Atlantic. It also includes Danish and Norwegian coastal waters.

Allied Command Europe is divided into the following subordinate commands:

(a) Allied Forces Central Europe has its headquarters in Fontainebleau and comprises 24 divisions (out of the required 30) assigned to the Supreme Commander as follows:

United Kingdom	3
United States	5 plus 3 armoured regiments
France	2
Germany	9 (3 more are being organized)
Belgium	2
Netherlands	2
Canada	1 brigade

The tactical air forces available include some 3,500 aircraft of which 500 plus US fighter-bombers and a smaller number of British *Canberras* have a nuclear capability and the range to cover important sections of eastern Russia. An integrated early-warning and air defence system has been developed for West Germany, the Low Countries, and N.E. France, of which an important element is 13 Army *Hawk* battalions.

The command is sub-divided into Northern Army Group and Central Army Group. Northern Army Group is responsible for defence of the sector north of – roughly speaking – the Gottingen – Liège axis. It includes the British and Benelux divisions, 3 of the German divisions, and the Canadian brigade. It is supported by 2nd Allied Tactical Air Force which is comprised of British, Dutch, Belgian, and German units. Other land forces are under CENTAG and other air forces under the corresponding air command – 4th ATAF.

So far 7 countries have contributed one or more reinforced infantry battalions to form a mobile task force. It is intended that this group should have nuclear weapons and organic air and sea transport. It is to serve as a reserve formation for NATO as a whole.

Central Europe is taken to include the

Heligoland Bight and so the command would control the German North Seas fleet and part of the Dutch navy in the event of war.

(b) Allied Forces Northern Europe has its headquarters at Kolsaas in Norway and is responsible for the defence of Norway, Denmark, Schleswig-Holstein and the Baltic approaches. All the Danish and Norwegian land, sea, and tactical air forces are earmarked for it. The Germans have assigned 1 division, 2 combat air wings, and their Baltic Navy. The division is counted as part of the Central European forces when assessing progress towards SACEUR's 30-division target.

(c) Allied Forces Southern Europe has its headquarters in Naples and is responsible for the defence of Italy, Greece and Turkey. The forces assigned include 14 divisions from Turkey, 8 from Greece, and 7 from Italy, as well as the tactical air forces of these countries which comprise some 1,000 warplanes. Various other divisions have been earmarked for AFSOUTH and so has the United States Sixth Fleet which would become Striking Force South if NATO became involved in war.

(d) Allied Forces Mediterranean has its headquarters in Malta and is primarily responsible for safeguarding communications in the Mediterranean and territorial waters of the Black Sea and for protecting the Sixth Fleet. The national fleets and maritime air forces of Italy, Greece, and Turkey, together with the British Mediterranean Fleet, are assigned to or earmarked for this command.

(2) Allied Command Atlantic

The duties of Supreme Allied Commander Atlantic in the event of war are (a) to participate in the strategic strike and (b) to protect sea communications from attack from submarines and aircraft. For these purposes the 8 NATO naval powers that border on the Atlantic have earmarked forces for exercises and, if need be, for war. SACLANT is responsible for the North Atlantic area north of the Tropic of Cancer including the northern North Sea. Three subordinate commands have been established – Western Atlantic Area, Eastern Atlantic Area, and Striking Force Atlantic. The striking force is provided by the United States Second Fleet with its 2 or 3 attack carriers.

There are probably about 450 escort vessels serving in the navies of the nations concerned of which a high proportion are wholly or partly designed for anti-submarine work. About 250 of these are normally serving outside the Atlantic area and a substantial fraction of the remainder would be undergoing repairs and refits at any one time. Most NATO navies are equipping and training their submarine forces primarily for ASW and well over 150 boats are potentially available in the Atlantic for such duties. The 8 nations in Allied Command Atlantic also have about 375 long-range land-based maritime patrol planes in operation, a large majority of which are stationed on or near Atlantic coasts. Furthermore the United States Navy alone has over 1,000 carrier-borne specialist anti-submarine fixed-wing aircraft and helicopters of which about half are embarked at any one time. Another 300 or so are serving in the other navies concerned. The overall total that could be quickly operational from carriers out on Atlantic sea stations is probably around 400.

All these estimates include units earmarked for Channel Command.

(3) The Channel Command

The role of Channel Command is to exercise maritime control of the English Channel and the southern North Sea. Many of the smaller warships of Belgium, France, the Netherlands and the United Kingdom are earmarked for this command as are some maritime aircraft.

NATIONAL FORCES

BELGIUM

General	Population: 9,200,000
	Length of military service: 18 months
	Total armed forces: 110,000 (34% conscripts)
	Defence Budget: $364,000,000
Army	Total strength: 85,000
	2 infantry divisions with M-47 tanks
	2 reserve divisions
Navy	Total strength: 5,000
	50 minesweepers
Air Force	Total strength: 20,000
	400 planes including 2 interceptor squadrons of CF-100 and 5 of *Hunter* 6 and 6 fighter-bomber squadrons of F-84Fs
	Some *Nike-Ajax* and *Honest John* missiles
	2 transport squadrons
	(All these forces are assigned to NATO)

CANADA

General	Population: 18,000,000
	Voluntary military service
	Total armed forces: 124,000
	Defence Budget: $1,589,000,000
Army	Total strength: 50,000
	1 brigade group of 6,500 men in Germany
	3 brigades in Canada (2 earmarked for NATO)
	43,000 militia
Navy	Total strength: 21,700
	1 16,000-ton carrier (partly A.S.)
	43 escorts
	1 submarine
	10 minesweepers
Air Force	Total strength: 52,500
	5 fighter squadrons in NORAD (see page 10)
	12 fighter squadrons in Europe, becoming 8 by early-1963. By late-1963 they will convert from

F-86s and CF-100s to 200 CF-104s

4 transport squadrons

4 maritime squadrons (3 *Argus* and 1 *Neptune*) earmarked for SACLANT

DENMARK

General Population: 4,600,000

Length of military service: 16 months (24 months for N.C.Os), becoming 12 months. Also reserve liability

Total armed forces: 46,500 plus 150,000 mobilizable reserves (excluding the volunteer Home Guard)

Defence Budget: $180,000,000

Army Total strength: 32,000

2⅔ armoured infantry brigades, each with 6,000 men in 5 battalions including one tank battalion with *Centurions*

4 reservist armoured infantry brigades could mobilize in 24 hours

2 *Honest John* battalions (with conventional warheads)

55,000 Army Home Guards for local defence

Navy Total strength: 7,000

18 escorts

3 submarines

8 minesweepers

13 other ships

Air Force Total strength: 7,500

200 warplanes in 3 F-100 and 3 F-86 squadrons and one *Hunter* squadron

1 *Nike-Ajax* battalion with 36 missiles

Some *Hawk* units to be established soon

FRANCE

General Population: 46,000,000

Length of military service: about 2 years—to be reduced to 18 months by March, 1963

Total armed forces: 705,000 by May 1963

Defence Budget: $3,531,000,000 (1962), $3,786,000,000 (1963)

Army Total strength: 500,000 by May 1963

The army is being reorganized. It will contain 6 divisions of which 2 will be in Germany assigned to NATO and 4 in France under national command. Each division will have 3 brigades of which one may be armoured. Tank regiments are equipped with M-48 battle tanks and AMX-13 light tanks. The army has 1,000 light planes and helicopters

The 2 NATO divisions in Germany include one mechanized and one armoured. Those in France will include one light armoured (equipped with AMX-13s) and one airborne, which is available for deployment overseas

France is organized into military districts for the training and mobilization of reservists. Over 2,000 men are in Berlin

Navy Total strength: 68,000

2 22,000-ton carriers ⎱ partly

1 11,000-ton carrier ⎰ A.S.

1 14,000-ton carrier

2 cruisers

86 escorts

19 submarines

111 minesweepers

The *Aeronavale* has 12 squadrons, including 6 of fighters. During 1962 it has received 40 *Etendard* IV and 45 more are ordered.

Air Force Total strength: 137,000

(a) Strategic Air Command (see page 10)

(b) 1st Tactical Air Force has 450 aircraft of which 75 are in Germany assigned to NATO. Since late-1961 *Mirage* IIIs (440 of which are ordered) have been entering service, in addition to other French-built aircraft, to replace F-84s, F-86s and F-100s

(*c*) Air Defence of the Territory:
10 squadrons of *Super Mysteres*
5 squadrons with 70 *Vautour* II Ns
Nike-Ajax units

(*d*) Transport Command with 200 *Noratlases*

GERMANY

General Population: 53,400,000

Length of military service: 18 months plus 9 months reserve full-time training liability up to the age of 45

Total armed forces: 353,000 (one-third conscripts), becoming 500,000 in a year or two. All except the Territorial Forces are assigned to NATO.

Defence Budget: $3,750,000,000

Army Total strength: 245,000 (350,000 planned ceiling by 1963/4)
5 armoured infantry divisions
2 armoured divisions
1 mountain division
1 airborne division
3 more armoured infantry divisions are being prepared. All divisions are being brought to 90% war establishment

Each division echelon has about 5,000 men in special units of A.A., field artillery, signals, engineers, etc. It normally contains 3 brigades. Grenadier brigades have 4,000 men and 50 tanks and armoured brigades 3,000 men and 100 tanks

The battle tank force includes 1,500 M-47s and approximately 1,000 M-48s

At divisional level *Honest John* missile battalions are maintained. Corps troops are to receive *Sergeant* for evaluation in 1963. 3 *Pershing* battalions should be operational under direct Army Group command by 1964

There is a Territorial Force of 22,000 men for staff and rear area duties

Navy Total strength: 25,000
1 Naval Air Wing (*Sea Hawks* and *Gannets*)
38 escorts
15 submarines
72 minesweepers
57 other ships

Air Force Total strength: 83,000 (100,000 planned ceiling)
7 fighter and fighter-bomber wings, 1 reconnaissance and 1 transport wing at 90-100% full strength. Eventually G-91s will replace F-84s and F-86s and also equip 3 more fighter/fighter-bomber wings and 3 more reconnaissance wings which, together with 2 more transport wings, are due to form by December, 1965
There are some *Hawk* and *Nike-Ajax* battalions

GREECE

General Population: 8,400,000

Length of military service: 24–30 months, followed by 19 years on the first-line reserve

Total armed forces: At least 160,000. The annual call-up is 55,000

Defence Budget: $170,000,000

Army Total strength: About 120,000, with a large first-line reserve
10 infantry divisions of which about 3 are close to full strength
A recently formed armoured division has M-47 battle tanks
8 divisions are NATO-assigned and the rest earmarked
Some *Honest John* batteries are in service

Navy Total strength: 17,000
1 cruiser
23 escorts

2 submarines
19 minesweepers
10 other ships

Air Force Total strength: 22,000
About 250 F-84s, F-86s and F-100s. Throughout 1962 G91s were entering service. F-104s are also being procured
Some *Nike-Ajax* units

ITALY

General Population: 51,000,000
Length of military service: 18 months for the Army and Air Force, 24 months for the Navy
Total armed forces: 470,000
Defence Budget: $1,255,000,000

Army Total strength: 370,000
5 infantry divisions (3 regiments in each)
5 alpine brigades
2 armoured divisions
2 *Honest John* battalions with M-47 tanks
Most of these formations are close to war establishment of 10 – 15,000. The rest would be filled out with reservists
The Carabinieri police could provide another 80,000 infantrymen
Most of these forces are earmarked for NATO
N.B. The US Southern European Task Force based on Vicenza has 2 *Corporal* and 2 *Honest John* battalions

Navy Total strength: 40,000
2 cruisers
49 escorts
6 submarines
114 minesweepers
3 other ships

Air Force Total strength: 60,000 in July 1963
7 air brigades of which 2 are fighter; these have F-84 Fs and F-86 Es but will convert to F-104 Gs, starting in 1962.

3 fighter-bomber 'aerobrigata' are replacing their F-84 Fs with G91s, 2 squadrons of which have already been formed
2 *Jupiter* squadrons, each with 15 missiles, have been formed.
A *Nike-Ajax* complex has been established near Venice
All combat elements are NATO assigned

LUXEMBOURG

General Population: 350,000
Length of military service: 9 months
Defence Budget: $7,000,000

Army Total strength: 5,500
A brigade would be available to NATO after mobilization

NETHERLANDS

General Population: 11,600,000
Length of military service: 20 – 24 months plus 15 years reserve liability
Total armed forces: 141,000
Defence budget: $555,000,000

Army Total strength: 98,000
2 mechanized divisions assigned to NATO
1 infantry division, 3 infantry brigades and army corps troops, to be formed by call-up of reservists, earmarked for NATO
Tank battalions are equipped with *Centurion* tanks
Some *Honest John* units

Navy Total strength: 23,000 including 4,000 Marines
1 16,000-ton carrier (partly for A.S.)
2 cruisers
35 escorts
6 submarines
68 minesweepers
7 amphibious craft

The Naval Air Arm includes 1 squadron of *Sea Hawks* and 5 anti-submarine and reconnaissance squadrons

Air Force Total strength: 20,000

16 squadrons, of which 9 are fighter squadrons (*Hunters* and F-86 Ks) 6 are fighter-bomber squadrons (F-84 Fs) and one is a reconnaissance squadron RF-84 F)

In the beginning of 1963 F-104 Gs will come into service

1 *Nike-Ajax* battalion in service and a second being formed

3 *Hawk* units will be formed in the near future

NORWAY

General Population: 3,600,000

Length of military service: 16 – 18 months

Total armed forces: 34,000

Defence budget: $191,000,000

Army Total strength: 18,000

2 brigades of which one (with an *Honest John* battery with conventional warheads) is in Arctic Norway

Mobilization could produce 9 reserve regiments, containing 75,000 men and Local Defence and Home Guard forces of 100,000 strong

Navy Total strength: 5,500

5 escorts
7 submarines
18 minesweepers
6 other ships

Air Force Total strength: 10,000

140 F-86 Fs and Ks in 8 tactical squadrons and 45 other aircraft

4 squadrons will start re-equipping with F-104s in early-1963

Some A.A. battalions, including one with *Nike-Ajax*

PORTUGAL

General Population: 9,150,000

Length of military service: 18 – 24 months for the Army, 36 for the Air Force, 48 for the Navy

Total armed forces: 80,000

Defence budget: $158,000,000

Army Total strength: 58,000 including 14,000 colonial troops. About 25,000 white troops remain in Angola (including one of the two divisions earmarked for NATO) and 10,000 in Mozambique

Navy Total strength: 9,300 plus 500 commandos

31 escorts
3 submarines
18 minesweepers

Air Force Total strength: 12,500 including parachute battalions. 350 aircraft including 2 F-86F squadrons and a *Neptune* squadron

TURKEY

General Population: 29,500,000

Length of military service: 2 years for the Army and Air Force, 3 years for the Navy

Total armed forces: 455,000

Defence budget: $287,000,000 (1961)

Army Total strength: 400,000. Mainly conscripts, but all the N.C.O's are regulars

16 divisions, mostly with 3 brigades each, and some independent brigades. (Altogether there are 6 armoured brigades, all with M-47 tanks.) All the divisions are NATO assigned

Honest John and *Nike-Ajax* rockets are in service

Plans exist to call up about 2,500,000 reservists if necessary, but they would chiefly serve in rear areas

Navy Total strength: 35,000
19 escorts
10 submarines
29 minesweepers
5 other ships

Air Force Total strength: 20,000
375 planes
3 F-100 squadrons
3 F-86 squadrons
9 F-84 F and G squadrons
1 15-missile *Jupiter* squadron
1 C-47 transport wing
50–100 F-104Gs will be procured between 1962 and 1965: 25 G-91s have been ordered

UNITED KINGDOM

General Population: 52,500,000
Voluntary military service
Total armed forces: 415,000 British and 30,000 Gurkha and colonial troops. 200,000 mobilizable reservists
Defence budget: $4,180,000,000

Army Total strength: 170,000 British troops
(*a*) Europe:
51.000 in 7 brigades in Germany (to be expanded to UK to 55,000) and 80,000 in UK including a strategic reserve of 3 brigades (2 earmarked for NATO). 3,000 men are stationed in Berlin. All but 2 of the tank regiments are in Europe. The chief battle tank is the *Centurion* (76, 83 or 105-mm. gun), but there are also *Conquerors* with 120-mm. guns. In 1963 *Chieftains* with 120-mm. guns will enter service. A complete armoured brigade includes 3 armoured regiments and one infantry battalion and has 120 tanks; an infantry brigade includes 3 infantry battalions and one armoured regiment and has 40 tanks
3 artillery regiments have *Honest John* and 8″ howitzers and 2 have *Corporal*

(*b*) Overseas:
Near East Command (Cyprus) includes 7 British infantry battalions; Middle East Command (Aden) includes 5 British infantry or airborne battalions and 5 local battalions (3–4,00 men); Far East Command (Singapore) includes 4 British infantry battalions and 7 Gurkha battalions
N.B. 2 battalions in the strategic reserve and one in Bahrein make up the Parachute Brigade

Navy Total strength: 100,000
(*a*) 2 44,000-ton carriers ⎤ all
1 30,000-ton carrier ⎬ partly
2 23,000-ton carriers ⎦ A.S.
2 commando carriers
5 cruisers
108 escorts
49 submarines (1 nuclear-powered)
45 minesweepers
There is an amphibious warfare squadron based on Aden which could provide 1–3 battalions
(*b*) The Fleet Air Arm has 13 strike and/or interceptor squadrons equipped with *Buccaneers*, *Sea Venoms*, *Sea Vixens* and 70 *Scimitars*. *Wessex* and *Whirlwind* anti-submarine helicopters are in service
(*c*) The Royal Marines maintain 5 commandos (i.e. battalions). 2 are based in UK, 2 in Singapore and 1 in Aden. One commando is in each commando ship

Air Force Total strength: 145,000
(*a*) Bomber Command (see page 9)
(*b*) Fighter Command has *Lightning* and *Javelin* interceptors and *Bloodhound* A.A. missiles. Can reinforce overseas commands

(c) Overseas Commands:
The RAF component in 2 ATAF (see page 12) is to receive some *Valiant* Bombers. RAF Commands based on Cyprus, Aden and Singapore corresponding to Army structure have *Shackleton* maritime reconnaissance squadrons, *Canberras*, *Javelins*, and (except in the Far East) *Hunters*

(d) Transport Command:
This is used for routine logistic support and to provide a military airlift. The 4-engine transport fleet includes 23 *Britannias*, 10 *Comets*, 20 *Argosies*, 48 *Hastings* and 32 *Beverleys*. It could lift 1,600 tons for 1,500 miles or 425 tons for 4,000 miles. 5 more *Comets* have been delivered and 36 more *Argosies* are on order

UNITED STATES

General　Population: 181,000,000
Length of military service: Selective service for 2 years, but over 90% of men serving are volunteers
Total armed forces: 2,815,000, becoming 2,680,000 by June, 1963. At present 440,000 are serving in the European theatre and 280,000 in the Pacific
Defence budget: $52,000,000,000

Army　Total strength: 1,080,000, becoming 950,000 by June, 1963
The Army today contains 16 combat-ready divisions (including 2 airborne and 2 armoured). A pentomic infantry division contains 13,700 men and its core is 5 infantry battle-groups each 1,450 strong. An armoured division totals 14,600 and includes 4 tank battalions and 4 armoured infantry battalions. Though pentomic divisions still predominate, conversion to a ROAD is proceeding rapidly; each ROAD division contains between 5 and 15 fighting battalions (armoured, armoured infantry, infantry and airborne being the types available). They are usually grouped into 3 brigades

The US VII Army of 5 Divisions and three armoured cavalry regiments is stationed in Germany. 5,000 men are stationed in Berlin. 3 divisions are stationed in the Far East.

The surface-to-surface nuclear weapons inventory is composed of *Davy Crockett* mortars, 8 in. howitzers and *Little John* and *Honest John* missiles within divisions, *Lacrosse*, *Corporal* and *Sergeant* missiles at corps level and *Pershing* and *Redstone* at field army level. Other equipment includes 1,000+ light aircraft and about 2,500 battle tanks. The units in Europe will have been largely re-equipped with the 50-ton M-60 tank (carrying a 105 mm. gun) by the end of 1963. Other troops will still predominantly use 44-ton M-48s with 90 mm. guns. In 1961 the Strategic Reserve Air Corps based in the continental USA was combined with Tactical Air Command to form the new Strike Command. STRAC now comprises 2 airborne, 2 armoured and 4 infantry divisions, of which one armoured and one infantry are National Guard divisions

The National Guard and Army Reserve is 700,000 strong. It is to be re-organized so as to be able to provide 2 combat-ready divisions within 5 weeks and an extra 6 divisions and 9 independent brigades 3 weeks later. These formations will come from a priority reserve of 465,000

Navy Total Strength: 660,000 (650,000 in June 1963)

850 operational ships (385 warships, 235 combatants and 230 auxiliaries) of which just under half are with the 1st and 7th Fleets. The 7th Fleet operates between 160 degrees East and the middle of the Indian Ocean and normally has 125 ships, including 3 attack carriers, on station. The 1st Fleet operates in the Eastern Pacific. The remaining ships of the USN, except for the ballistic submarines, are with the 2nd Fleet in the Atlantic and the 6th Fleet in the Mediterranean. The 6th Fleet is comprised of 50 ships including 3 attack carriers. Of the total number of ships 57 per cent were completed before 1947

The aircraft inventory, including Marine Corps planes, is 7,400 of which 60 per cent are combat machines. They include well over 1,000 A4D *Skyhawks*, 700+ F8U *Crusaders*, 400 F4D *Skyrays*, and about 150 A3D *Skywarriors*. The 500 F3H *Demons* produced are being replaced by the F4H *Phantom* 2s of which about 200 have so far been produced. The A3J *Vigilante* is also now joining the fleet. The 1,000+ anti-submarine aircraft being employed include the land-based P2V-7 *Neptune* and P3V-1 *Orion* and the carrier-based S2F *Tracker* and HSS-1 and HSS-2 helicopters

The active fleet includes:

1	75,000-ton nuclear-powered attack carrier
6	60,000-ton attack carriers
3	51,000-ton attack carriers
7	33,000-ton attack carriers
9	30,000-ton anti-submarine carriers
15	cruisers
225	escorts
9	ballistic submarines
105	general purpose submarines (of which 16 are nuclear-powered)

There are 110,000 reservists available to commission some of the 750 inactive naval vessels still preserved in the 'mothball' fleet and/or to bring other ships to wartime manning levels

Marine Corps The 190,000 Marines provide 3 divisions with organic air wings of 3–400 planes apiece. One division-wing is based in N. Carolina, one in California and the third in Okinawa. The 50,000 Marine reservists could fill out a fourth division, at present kept in embryonic form. USN amphibious shipping is permanently allotted to the Marine Corps and distributed among the division-wings on a proportionate basis. It can provide a 2-division simultaneous lift. The 6th and 7th Fleets each have one reinforced battalion of 2,000 men permanently embarked

Air Force Total strength: 885,000, becoming 860,000 by July 1963.

There are 90 wings; a bomber wing generally contains 45 aircraft and a fighter wing 75.

Strategic Air Command and NORAD. (See pages 9 and 10)

General purpose forces:
The combat elements consist of B-57 and B-66 bomber squadrons and of 16 tactical wings flying F-84Fs, F-100s, F-104s and F-105s. The first F-110s (USAF version of the F4H) are becoming operational; by July 1963, 300 are to have been produced

The greater part of these general purpose forces has been assigned to Tactical Air Command which has 16 wings and 50,000 men; 6 of the wings are tactical fighters and two of them are normally on rotational duty in Europe. Other wings include 220 transport and aerial tankers which, aided by the SAC in-flight refuelling tanker force, can enable composite Air Strike Forces of up to 300 warplanes to deploy halfway across the world in 48 hours. 5 new TAC wings are being created

The Military Air Transportation Service:

This provides logistic support and a military airlift. Its fleet of 4-engined transports suitable for airlift purposes consists of 112 C-118s, 62 C-121s, 329 C-124s, 25 C-130Es, 46 C-133s and 44 C-135s. By March 1963 there will be 50 C-130Es

The Air Force Ready Reserve and Air National Guard numbers 140,000 of whom half are attached to TAC. However, they have recently surrendered 300 F-84Fs and F-104s to the regular forces. There are a further 400,000 men in the Air Force Reserve available for call up

CENTRAL TREATY ORGANIZATION

The members of CENTO are Pakistan, Iran, Turkey (p. 17) and the United Kingdom (p.18). The United States is an associate member, but is represented on the co-ordinating Council of military deputies and on the economic and counter-subversion committees. CENTO does not have an international command structure nor are forces allocated to it.

NATIONAL FORCES

IRAN

General	Population: 21,000,000
	Length of military service: 2 years
	Total armed forces: 200,000
	Defence budget: $125,000,000, but may be cut heavily
Army	Total strength: 208,000. Plans to expand to 250,000 in 1962 have been abandoned. The present figure may soon be reduced
	12 divisional organizations exist. There are M-47, *Sherman* and T-34 tanks
	A paramilitary gendarmerie of 30,000
Navy	Total strength: 1,000
	2 escorts
	2 minesweepers
	2 other ships
Air Force	Total strength: 7,500
	About 150 planes including one tactical wing of 75 F-84G/86s and some F-47D *Thunderbolt*
	This will receive 100 more US

aircraft including 60 fighters and some transports

PAKISTAN

General	Population: 96,000,000
	Voluntary military service
	Total armed forces: 253,000
	Defence budget: $210,000,000
	US Military Aid: $1,100,000,000 from 1954 to 1962
Army	Total strength: 230,000
	8 divisions organized on a triangular basis and equipped with *Patton* tanks
	250,000 lightly armed militia and about 30,000 Ayad Kashmir troops
Navy	Total strength: 7,700
	7 escorts
	6 minesweepers
Air Force	Total strength: 15,000
	1 squadron of 7 B-57 *Canberra* bombers
	1 squadron of 12 F-104s

SOUTH-EAST ASIA TREATY ORGANIZATION

The members of SEATO are Australia, France, New Zealand, Pakistan, the Philippines, Thailand, the United Kingdom and the United States. They are committed to build up collective economic and military strength and to consult with a view to joint defensive action in the event of direct or indirect aggression against a member or against the 'designated states' of Laos, Cambodia and South Vietnam. The area is the South-West Pacific theatre South of 21° 30' N. There is no central command structure and forces remain under national control. The largest Western base in the West Pacific is that on Okinawa with 42,000 US servicemen. The 28th Commonwealth Brigade plus supporting air units is available in Malaya but the Federal Government has indicated that it would not necessarily accord base facilities for SEATO operations.

The only large scale fighting going on in the SEATO area at the moment is in South Vietnam where a 200,000 strong government army with 7,000 American advisers is combatting the Viet-cong guerillas.

NATIONAL FORCES

AUSTRALIA

General   Population: 10,500,000
Voluntary military service
Total armed forces: 48,500
Defence budget: $472,000,000

Army   Total strength: 21,600 (plus 22,500 Citizen Military Forces)
1 infantry battalion with artillery support in Malaya
1 *Centurion* tank regiment
2 battle groups (reinforced infantry battalions)
1 Pacific Island Regiment battalion
8 CMF battle groups

Navy   Total strength: 11,100
1 16,000-ton carrier (partly A.S.)
1 carrier (fast transport)
13 escorts
6 minesweepers
About 100 naval aircraft, including *Sea Venoms* and *Gannets*

Air Force   Total strength: 16,000 plus 900 CMF
3 *Canberra* squadrons
4 F-86 squadrons (1 to convert to *Mirage* IIIs in 1963)
2 *Neptune* patrol squadrons
3 transport squadrons (1 *Hercules* and 2 *Dakota*)
450 aircraft altogether
Bloodhound AA missiles

NEW ZEALAND

General   Population: 2,400,000
Voluntary military service
Total armed forces: 12,200
Defence budget: $81,000,000

Army   Total strength: 4,900
1 brigade, including a battalion in Malaya

Navy   Total strength: 2,900
1 cruiser
4 escorts

Air Force   Total strength: 4,400
1 bomber squadron with 12 *Canberras*
1 maritime reconnaissance squadron
3 transport squadrons

PHILIPPINE REPUBLIC

General   Population: 25,000,000
Voluntary military service
Total armed forces: 32,000 plus a paramilitary National Police
Defence budget: $100,000,000

Army   Total strength: 22,000
Has M-41 tanks

Navy   Total strength: 4,000
14 escorts
2 minesweepers

Air Force   Total strength: 6,250
4 squadrons of F-86s (1 carrying *Sidewinders*)

THAILAND

General Population: 26,000,000
Length of military service: 2 years
Total armed forces: 134,000 plus
30,000 militarized police
Defence budget: $70,000,000
US Military Aid: $400,000,000
to 1962

Army Total strength: 90,000
3 infantry divisions (nominally
with 3 brigades each) and 1
composite division with armour

Navy Total strength: 18,000 plus 4,000
marines
5 escorts
4 minesweepers
24 small ships

Air Force Total strength: 22,000
About 350 aircraft including
about 150 first-line
First-line includes 30 F-84Gs and
F-86s; more F-86s are being
procured

US MUTUAL DEFENSE TREATIES

Those countries which have Mutual Defense
Treaties with the United States are Japan,
Formosa, and South Korea.
Their forces are as follows:

SOUTH KOREA

General Population: 23,000,000
Voluntary military service
Total armed forces: 602,000
Defence budget: $130,000,000
US Military Aid: $1,800,000,000
to date

Army Total strength: 570,000
29 divisions
12,000 Koreans serve in the
2-division American garrison

Navy Total strength: 17,000
18 escorts
10 minesweepers

Air Force Total strength: 15,000
About 300 planes including two
wings of 150 F-86F fighter-
bombers and two squadrons of
F-86D interceptors

TAIWAN

General Population: 10,050,000
Length of military service: 2 years
and reserve liability
Total armed forces: 570,000
Defence budget: $230,000,000
US Military Aid: $1,800,000,000
1952–62

Army Total strength: 400,000 including
70,000 on Quemoy and Matsu

21 infantry divisions
2 armoured divisions
1 *Nike-Hercules* battalion

Navy Total strength: 35,000 plus 27,000
marines
35 escorts
12 minesweepers
2 other ships
Amphibious shipping for one
division is available

Air Force Total strength: 110,000
3 interceptor wings of F-86Fs
(with *Sidewinders*) and F-104s
1 F-100 fighter-bomber wing
Each wing has about 75 planes.
Total of 5–600 planes including
400 first-line

JAPAN

General Population: 94,640,000
Voluntary military service
Total armed forces: 235,000
Defence budget: $569,000,000
US Military Aid: About
$800,000,000 since 1950

Army Total strength: 171,500 (planned
expansion to 180,000 with
30,000 reserves by 1967)
13 divisions of 7–9,000 men each
organized into 4 battle groups
1 division, based on Hokkaido,
is mechanized
The Army has 271 light aircraft
and helicopters and 900
American-built tanks including
M-41s

Navy Total strength: 24,500
44 escorts
3 submarines
100 anti-submarine aircraft
The naval air component has about 200 aircraft including helicopters

Air Force Total strength: 39,000
2 tactical wings
4 fighter-interceptor wings
A total of 1,000 aircraft of which 550 are jets

The first of 180 F-104Js have been accepted; they will partially replace 100 F-86Ds and 350 F-86Fs in service. The F-104s and 280 of the F-86Fs are to have *Sidewinders*

The first wing of 72 *Nike-Ajax* missiles and 36 launchers is operational in the Tokyo and Yokohama areas. The second will enter service in 1963 as will some *Hawk* batteries

TABLE I MANPOWER, DEMOGRAPHY AND MONEY

Country	Total Armed Forces (Regular)	As Percentage of Male Labour Force	Population Density per Sq. Km.	No. of Cities of over 200,000 Inhabitants	Defence Budget as Percentage of National Income*	Country
Belgium	110,000	4.33	301.3	4	3.76	
Canada	124,000	2.58	1.80	9	5.61	
Denmark	46,500	3.18	106.88	1	3.23	
France	705,000	5.33	83.39	8	7.20	
Germany	353,000	2.20	215.36	26	5.91	
Greece	160,000	6.24	64.16	2	5.77	
Italy	470,000	2.84	169.31	14	4.43	
Luxembourg	5,500	4.95	135.14	—	1.71	
Netherlands	141,000	4.23	345.13	4	5.00	
Norway..	34,000	2.92	11.11	1	5.00	
Portugal	80,000	2.89	99.49	2	6.93	
Turkey	455,000	5.14	38.46	4	4.34	
United Kingdom ..	415,000	2.47	215.0	21	6.67	
United States	2,815,000	5.68	19.69	61	11.25	
TOTAL NATO ..	5,914,000	4.22	21.8	157		
Australia	48,500	1.45	1.36	6	3.22	
Iran	208,000	3.29	12.8	5	—	
New Zealand	12,200	1.77	8.93	3	2.40	
Pakistan	253,000.	0.87	101.62	6	4.09	
Philippines	32,000	0.49	83.42	2	3.03	
Thailand	135,000	1.99	50.58	1	2.56	
TOTAL WESTERN ALLIANCES ..	6,603,000	3.43	19.8	180		
Japan	235,000	0.89	255.1	37	1.41	
S. Korea	602,000	12.82	230.85	4	8.20	
Taiwan	570,000	23.34	279.32	4	9.00	
TOTAL US TREATY POWERS	8,010,000	3.54	23.27	225		
	29,500	5.14	59.15	—	—	Albania
	120,000	4.81	71.22	1	4.5†	Bulgaria
	185,000	5.04	115.36	4	—	Czechoslovakia
	85,000	1.79	158.4	5	2.5†	East Germany
	80,500	2.66	108.53	1	1.8†	Hungary
	257,000	3.1	96.47	9	3.7†	Poland
	222,000	3.68	77.71	1	—	Roumania
	3,600,000	5.5	9.74	76	8.09‡	USSR
	4,579,000	4.86	13.55	97	—	TOTAL WARSAW PACT
	2,400,000	1.12	73.44	50(est)	4.4†	China
	338,000	13.74	175.18	1	—	N. Korea
	260,000	6.6	90.72	2	—	N. Vietnam
	93,000	4.5	59.39	2	—	Cuba
	7,670,000	2.42	31.76	152		TOTAL COMMUNIST BLOC

NOTES.—*Based on an estimated figure of national income for 1962.

†These are 1959 figures submitted to the recent UN Committee on the economic consequences of disarmament.

‡Based on Defence Budget of 14,740 million US dollars. On the more realistic figure of 33,000 million US dollars, the percentage is **18.66.**

TABLE II

SOME COMPARATIVE ESTIMATES OF STRATEGIC STRENGTH
EARLY 1963

CATEGORY	WESTERN ALLIANCES	COMMUNIST BLOC
ICBMs (over 2,000 mile range)	450-500	75+
MRBMs (700–2,000 mile range)	250	700
Long-range bombers (over 5,000 mile range)	630	200
Medium-range bombers (over 2,000 mile range, including major carrier-based aircraft)	1,630	1,400
Battleships and carriers	40 (36)	—
Nuclear submarines*	32	12
Conventional submarines..	212 (48)	445 (50)
Cruisers	29 (31)	20 (10)
Escorts	842 (265)	124 (365)
Tanks†	16,000	38,000
Mobilized manpower (excluding paramilitary forces)	8,000,000 men	7,700,000 men

Ships in reserve are shown in brackets.
*Includes both missile and hunter submarines.
†Includes many obsolescent types.

177

TABLE III MAJOR NUCLEAR DELIVERY SYSTEMS 1962–3

(A) AIRCRAFT

Name	Origin	Best Range (Miles)	Speed Mach No. (mph)		All-up Weight (lb)	Became Operational	Typical Warload
B-52A-G..	USA	10,000	0.88	(665)	450,000	1955-61	2 *Hound Dog* ASMs in C and G, others H-bombs
B-52H	USA	12,500	0.88	(665)	488,000	1962	*Skybolt*
Bison	USSR	6,050	0.85	(600)	400,000+	1956	ASMs
TU-20 *Bear*	USSR	7,000	0.78	(580)	320,000	1956*	H-bomb
Vulcan B1 and B2 ..	UK	3,500	0.95	(630)	200,000	1957	*Blue Steel* in B2
Victor B1 and B2 ..	UK	3,500	0.95	(630)	200,000	1958	,, ,,
B-47	USA	3,200	0.83	(650)	200,000	1952	H-bomb
Valiant	UK	4,500	0.84	(567)	175,000	1955	45,000 lb
TU-16 *Badger*	USSR	3,500	0.87	(610)	170,000	1955*	ASM
B-58 *Hustler*	USA	2,000+	2.1	(1,385)	163,000	1960	H-bomb
Blinder	USSR	—	1.5	(1,030)	150,000	1962	ASM
A3D-2 *Skywarrior* ..	USA	3,000	0.83	(610)	73,000	1956	12,000 lb
Mirage IV	France	2,500	2.3	(1,520)	66,000	1964	Fission-bomb
Canberra B(L)8	UK	3,800	0.83	(580)	56,000	1955	15,000 lb
Flashlight	USSR	2,000	1.05	(690)	52,000	—	Fission-bomb
A3J *Vigilante*	USA	2,000	1.1	(700)	60,000	1961	H-bomb (e.g.)
F-105D *Thunderchief* ..	USA	2,000+	2.15	(1,420)	48,000	1961	9,700 lb including H-bombs
Buccaneer S.1	UK	3,860	1.05	(720)	46,000	1962	H-bomb
F-4H *Phantom II* ..	USA	2,000+	2.6	(1,504)	45,000	1962	11,000 lb
Scimitar	UK	1,500	0.97	(710)	40,000	1958	4,000 lb
F-100D *Super Sabre* ..	USA	1,500	1.3	(864)	35,000	1957	7,500 lb
F-104 *Starfighter* ..	USA	2,200	2.2	(1,450)	27,000	1958	4,200 lb
F-84F *Sabre*	USA	2,500	0.9	(650)	25,000	1954	6,000 lb
A4D-2 *Skyhawk* ..	USA	3,200	0.9	(685)	18,000	1956	5,000 lb

ASM = Air-to-Surface Missile.
*Earlier marks now obsolete.
The inconsistency between Mach numbers and speed in m.p.h. is accounted for by difference in operational ceilings.

(B) MISSILES—GROUND-TO-GROUND

Name	Propellant (†)	Launching Weight (lb)	Range in (S) Miles	Operational	Notes
USA					
Atlas (E)	L	260,000	9,000+	1959	3-megaton warhead
Titan I	L	220,000	9,000+	1961	4-megaton warhead
Minuteman	S	65,000	6,300	1962	600-kiloton warhead
Thor	L	110,000	1,725	1958	Obsolescent
Jupiter	L	110,000	1,725	1959	
Polaris A1	S	28,000	1,380	1960	600-kiloton warhead
Matador	S	10,000	500	1955	Obsolescent
Mace A and B	S	14,000	650	1960	*Mace* B has range of up to 1,380 miles
Regulus I	T & S	14,500	575	1955	Obsolescent
Pershing	S	35,000	300+	1962	Fully mobile
Redstone	L	61,000	200	1956	Obsolescent
Sergeant	S	10,000	85	1962	20-kiloton warhead
Corporal	L	12,000	75	1955	Obsolescent
USSR					
ICBM	L	300,000	8,000+	1955	10-megaton warhead
ICBM	SL	—		1963	
MRBM	L	122,000	2,100	1959	
MRBM	L	—	1,100	1961	
MRBM	—	—	700		
SSLM*	S	—	400	1959	
SSLM*	S	—	100	1959	
SRM *(Scud)*	L	—	120	1957	Ballistic
SRM *(Shaddock)*	T	—	175-350	1961	Cruise

†L = Liquid fuel
S = Solid fuel
SL = Storable liquid fuel
T = Turbojet
*SSLM = Submarine surface-launched Missile.
SRM = Short-range missile

179